BRITAIN'S RAILWAY MUSEUMS

Overleaf: *Supreme among earlier ornamental relics to be found in Clapham Museum is this magnificent candelabrum, in silver and crystal, presented to Robert Stephenson in 1839. At the base, three groups of cherubs are involved with diagrams of the origin of the steam engine, a beam engine and Stephenson's latest locomotive; higher, the figure of Minerva is shown demonstrating the application of steam to the purpose of locomotion while the whole is crowned with an ebullience of fluted curves representing the billowing expansion of the magical vapour itself.*

BRITAIN'S RAILWAY MUSEUMS

Peter Williams

LONDON

IAN ALLAN LTD

First published 1974

ISBN 0 7110 0565 6

Published by Ian Allan Ltd, Shepperton, Surrey,
and printed in the United Kingdom by
Ian Allan (Printing) Ltd.

Contents

Acknowledgements

The author wishes to express his gratitude to the following for their kind co-operation in allowing him to take and publish the photographs included in this book.

Curator of Historic Relics
British Railways Board
Museum of British Transport
Clapham.

The Railway Museum
York.

Keeper of Technology
Museum of Transport
Glasgow.

Chief Librarian and Curator
Great Western Railway Museum
Swindon.

The Director
The Science Museum
South Kensington.

Keeper of Technology
Museum of Technology for the East Midlands
Leicester.

The Director
Museum of Science and Industry
Birmingham.

Foreword

The function of the Transport Trust, of which I am President, is to help, encourage and co-ordinate the preservation of transport relics, so I welcome this book on Britain's railway museums.

The book has arrived at the right moment for never has interest in railway preservation been greater than it is now whether directed to exhibits in museums or to live items in action.

Two events make the appearance of this book timely. The first is the 150th anniversary of the opening of the Stockton & Darlington Railway, in September 1975, at which a steam-driven replica of George Stephenson's 'Locomotion' will perform. The second is the opening of the National Railway Museum in new premises at York, also planned for September 1975, which will combine the exhibits of the Clapham and York museums which are described and illustrated so fully in this book.

There is no shortage of interesting railway material available in this country—in some areas of the subject there is possibly too much— but it is desirable that the importance of railway preservation should be kept to the front of people's minds so that in future no neglect or indifference will be allowed to destroy what we have.

This book is a helpful reminder of some of the treasures we still possess.

Sir Peter Allen

THE IRON HORSE.

By G. BENFIELD, Engine Driver, Derby.

Printed to commemorate the satisfactory arrangement arrived at between the Directors of the Midland Railway Company and the Engine Drivers and Firemen in their employ, April 2nd, 1867.

The squire may boast of his prancing steed,
   As docile, swift, and free,
Easy to ride, gentle to guide,
   But the "Iron Horse" for me.

The lord may praise his racing pet,
   As graceful and swift as the fawn;
Her feet so neat, her coat so sleek,
   The most spirited ever born.

The farmer tells of the feats of strength
   That his steed in the shaft can do,
With limbs so round and health so sound,
   With joy his toil pursue.

But my song I'll raise to the "Iron Horse,"
   Whose back it's my lot to ride;
For strength and speed she's a bonny steed,
   Surpassing all beside.

She seems to rejoice to make her escape
   From her stable so dark with smoke,
And the grooms they stand, a happy band,
   Cracking the merry joke.

She screams, and hisses, and pants,
   And longs to be set to her task,
With a tender of coal, on the rail she doth roll,
   And the bridges like spectres fly past.

O'er hill and dale my steed I ride,
   Through gored rock and mountain,
Where the lamb is seen by the rippling stream,
   Or at the babbling fountain.

Her feet are swift and shod with steel,
   And seldom known to fail;
Right happy are we our steed to see
   Glide o'er the smooth-faced rail.

Her heart is set in a copper case,
   And is made of glowing coals,
And through her veins flies the rushing flames,
   As on the rail she rolls.

She's like a giant in her strength,
   With muscles made of brass,
Her sinews of steel that will not yield,
   And a coat as smooth as glass.

And though my steed is a ponderous weight,
   In a moment my will she'll obey;
And off she will rush with a gentle touch,
   And as quickly brought to stay.

Howe'er begrimmed with grease and smoke,
   He who in the saddle rides,
The physical mind of the huge steam Horse,
   In this faithful man abides.

My *footman* rides in a break behind
   And a faithful guard is he,
Should danger he spy with his watchful eye,
   A signal he'll give to me.

'Tis true, I am highly honored
   In my journeys far and wide,
For at junction and at station, *livery* servants in
   rotation,
   Stand my "Iron Horse" to guide.

'Tis true, the risk to life and limb
   Of my calling's very great,
For some she hath touched with her iron clutch,
   And death has been their fate.

And many a strong and hearty youth,
   By wet and sad exposure,
In a few short years, with bitter tears,
   Has filled a dark enclosure.

Exposed am I when the frowning sky
   Is drenching the earth with rain,
When the howling blast, with the thunder's crash
   And the red-winged light'ning's flame

And when the frost-king comes, with garment
   white,
   And covers all nature o'er,
And the frozen stream in the sun doth gleam,
   And the rill is set to the core.

'Tis then I feel convinced, by *cold*,
   Ten hours a day is plenty,
As much as He would have me do
   Who to this world hath sent me.

When the sun is high in the vaulted sky,
   And the balmy breeze is asleep,
And along the glade to the silent shade,
   The bleating cattle creep.

'Tis then I feel convinced, by *heat*,
   Ten hours a day is plenty,
As much as He would have me do
   Who to this world hath sent me.

Then while we at our dangerous craft
   Toil for our daily bread,
Oh, let us seek that God may keep
   His watch-guard o'er our head.

Then should misfortune on our path,
   Cast her shades of gloom,
May grace to help from that land be sent
   Where flowers eternal bloom.

With heads as clear as water bright,
   Hearts free from ostentation,
Oh, let us live prepared to die
   With Christ for our salvation.

WM. HALL, PRINTER, VICTORIA STREET, DERBY.

YORK

1   *On the model scene at York, a strong regional flavour was naturally apparent. One of the models most popular with visitors was this 5in gauge miniature of the streamlined A4 class Pacific No 2509 Silver Link, the first of Sir Nigel Gresley's show-stoppers for the LNER on the Newcastle to London run.*

2   *The cut-away boiler and firebox model reveals many interesting secrets of locomotive construction not normally visible on the real thing. Through the cut-out in the firebox wrapper can be seen the inner firebox wall; the part between the plates is known as the water space and is necessary so that the firebox is always surrounded by water which prevents burning of the plates. The large number of rivetted stays are positioned to brace one wall against the other. The boiler cut-away reveals the boiler tubes which carry the hot gases from the fire, and inside these tubes are the superheater elements; steam passing through these picks up even more heat and is dried to make it capable of greater expansion when it reaches the cylinders.*

3   *Mural exhibits included a map of the North Eastern Railway network in ceramic tiles and a wide selection of locomotive nameplates, many honouring prominent railway personalities from the north. From Mr Peppercorn's A1 class Pacific design come W. P. Allen (No 60114) Patrick Stirling (No 60119) Sir Vincent Raven (No 60126) and Auld Reekie (No 60160); A. H. Peppercorn LNER No 525 then BR No 60525 from that designers' improvement of Mr Thompson's A2 class Pacific; Sir Ronald Matthews (LNER No 4500 then No 1 then BR No 60001) and Sir Murrough Wilson (LNER No 4499 then No 2 then BR No 60002) were streamlined Gresley A4 class Pacifics, while A. Harold Bibby was Mr Thompson's 4-6-0 B1 class No 61250.*

4   *The makers plates which were on display span the years of the LNER's existence and recall the works at Doncaster, Gateshead, Darlington and Gorton together with contractor's names like Hawthorn Leslie, Armstrong-Whitworth and Beyer-Peacock.*

5   *One of the stationary steam engines displayed at York was this large-jet condensing beam engine from Ducie Street Manchester; in common with other large engines in the Museum, the lower portion of the flywheel unfortunately had to be removed to permit installation. Nameplates from the A1 Pacific class of the LNER-cum-BR honour Edward Fletcher (No 60142) Wilson Worsdell (No 60127) Archibald Sturrock (No 60118) and Foxhunter (No 60134).*

6   *Reconstructed in the smaller hall were four spans of the first iron railway bridge ever built anywhere in the world. The complete structure carried a horse-drawn portion of the Stockton and Darlington Railway over the River Gaunless between Brussleton and Etherley; the elliptical span members are a shapely feature later to appear on a grander scale in Brunel's Royal Albert Bridge at Saltash.*

7   *A novel method of displaying the cast iron station nameplates, originally fitted to the top rail of station bench seats, was on this short staircase leading to an upper storeroom.*

8   *In a veritable forest of lever frames and signalling apparatus can be traced the fascinating history of the control of rail traffic and the development of mechanical aids to safety on the track. Signal box equipment includes tablet and staff apparatus and level-crossing gate mechanisms.*

9   *In the days before the arrival of the locomotive, horses were used on the railway as the source of power; where gradients were sharp, particularly on mineral lines, it was soon discovered that a more efficient performance could be obtained from the animal if it were rested on the downhill journeys. A special vehicle, the Dandy Cart, was therefore provided in which the horse could enjoy the breeze and the run downhill while the train descended under gravity.*

10   *Viewed through the severed flywheel of a horizontal steam engine can be seen the Stockton and Darlington Dandy Cart, complete with mahogany Dobbin, a Chaldron Wagon, and a sectioned brake van in which the workings of an early 'Cord Communication' system can be seen.*

5

6

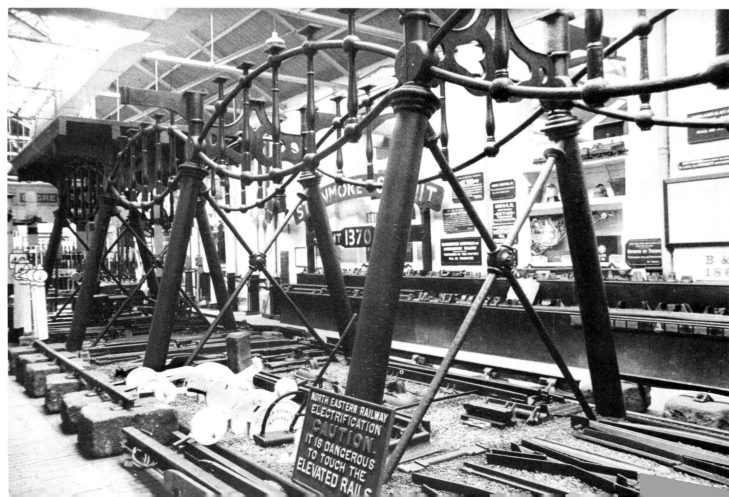

9

10

11 The Bodmin and Wadebridge Railway provided a choice of passenger accommodation as these Open Third and Closed Second examples show. Dating probably from the 1830s they illustrate the scant comfort available to the early rail traveller but, in view of the fact that his previous journey would have been made on foot or on horseback, he would doubtless be happy enough to be riding the railway at all, however spartan his surroundings. He did at least have a seat to sit on, unlike the previous type of Stanhope vehicle which was simply a box on wheels; the name apparently derived from the nickname given to them by the travelling public—there was no room to sit down, only stan' up.

12 The memory of the linen-draper from York who went on to earn for himself the title of 'The Railway King', George Hudson, is perpetuated in this marble bust. Heir to a considerable fortune, he saw railway mania as an opportunity to exercise his powerful drive and personality and energetically set about connecting York with the North Midland Railway thus completing the link to London. Other enterprises followed, he became Mayor of York, he accepted directorships and chairmanships and was later elected MP for Sunderland, but by this time certain events had led to an enquiry into his affairs as a result of which he was sent to prison and died a poor man.

13 The Hetton Colliery 0-4-0 locomotive was built in the pit workshops by George Stephenson and Nicholas Wood in 1822. Incorporating two vertical cylinders with connecting rods direct to crankpins on the driving wheels, the design obviated the need for intermediate gearing which had previously been considered necessary. Rebuilding took place in 1857 and 1882 and the locomotive was withdrawn from service in

1908, but all that complicated superstructure hissed into living motion again in 1925 when the Stockton and Darlington Centenary Cavalcade was proudly led by this ten ton veteran.

14 In 1812, when Mr Blenkinsop brought his locomotive into service at the Middleton Colliery, Leeds, it was not accepted that smooth wheels and smooth rails could produce sufficient propulsive traction to enable a locomotive to haul a load. His driven axle therefore featured these large-diameter spur wheels engaging in a rack outside the rail while the two other axles fitted with flanged wheels were not driven.

15 The first locomotive to run on rails in the USA was the Stourbridge Lion, built in 1828 and almost identical to The Agenoria seen here, built by Foster Rastrick, Stourbridge, the following year. Another two-cylinder design driving direct on to the wheels, a feature, incidentally, which does not allow spring suspension to be fitted, this locomotive was built for the Earl of Dudley's Shutt End Colliery Railway, Kingswinford, Staffs. The chimney is of great length and rises over 20ft amid the rafters of the entrance hall.

16 Alongside The Agenoria stands the Stockton and Darlington Railway First and Second Class composite Coach—truly a stage coach on rails. All the features of the road vehicle are there, the wood panelling and decorative mouldings, the roof rack complete with contemporary luggage, and the travelling porters draughty perch. Notice that passengers travelling First Class (centre compartment) are provided with windows in the coach side as well as in the door.

YORK

Plate 1
Above left: GNR 4-4-2 No 251
Left: NER Aerolite
Above: Signals & Levers

YORK

Plate 2
Above: Driving Wheel No 910
Above right: NER 4-4-0 No 1621
Right: 8ft Single GNR No 1

11

12

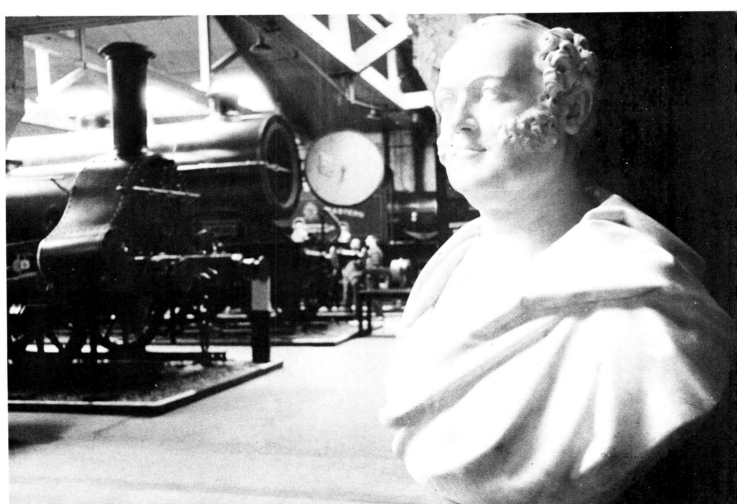

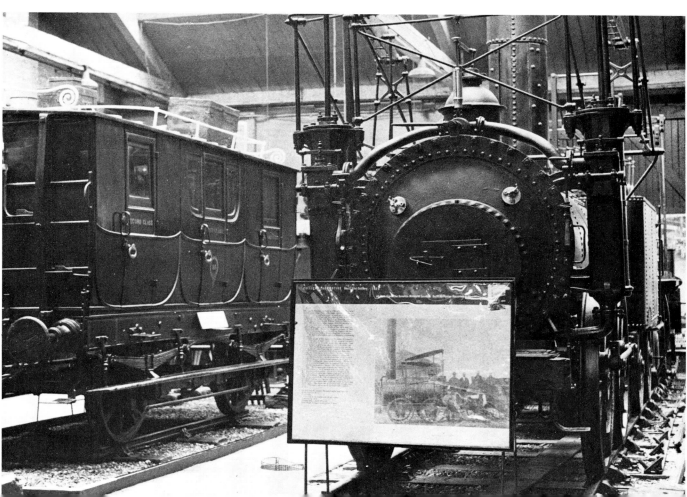

17   The North Eastern Railway locomotive No 66
18   named Aerolite is a specimen which has had as
varied a history as one could imagine. The original
Aerolite was constructed in 1851 and put on show
at the Great Exhibition of that year as a 2-2-2
well-tank; rebuilt in 1869 and later, after an
extensive rebuild in 1892 by William Worsdell as a
Von Borries two-cylinder compound, No 66 sported
a 4-2-2 wheel arrangement and an improved
appearance. The fourth and final rebuild came in 1902
when the locomotive acquired the form it has today, as
a trim 2-2-4 tank, although one wonders if the front
end would be visually more attractive were it a 4-2-2.
Before being retired in 1933 Aerolite became very
much a special locomotive and spent much of its later
life hauling official saloons.

19   Patrick Stirling's Eight-Foot Single of the Great
20   Northern Railway is considered by many to be the
22   most beautiful type of steam locomotive ever built;
22   this, together with the fact that the class produced
the most powerful express locomotives of their day,
makes No 1 an absorbing exhibit. As the eye takes
in the gracious sweep of the smokebox and cylinder,
the bold splasher and the arched running plate, the
functional cab, the safety valve cover that is just the
right shape and the noble chimney that is just the
right height, one sees Stirling as the talented artist.
Yet when one considers that in the 1880s these
locomotives hauled the fastest express trains anywhere
in the world at 70 and 75mph and even, during the
Railway Race to the North in 1895, hustled the

Aberdeen Sleeper the 105½ miles from King's Cross
to Grantham in 101 minutes, one sees Stirling as the
accomplished engineer. No 1, watched over by the
designer himself, was built in 1870 and was followed
by 52 others of the class; from its domeless boiler to
its square section wheel spokes it is every inch a
thoroughbred.

23   Known as the 'long-boilered goods', this 0-6-0 tender
24   locomotive was to the original concept of Robert
25   Stephenson, designed by William Bouch and built by
26   Dubs & Co of Glasgow for the Stockton and
Darlington Railway in 1874. The virtue of having
a long boiler extending over the coupled wheelbase was
that it enabled the firebox to be designed free of
restrictions imposed by adjacent running gear, although
in this example with a grate area of only 13.3sq ft
this freedom was apparently not exploited to the full.
As the fierce draught needed to make a long boiler
steam freely was a function of the grate area, these
locomotives were disappointing performers when used
for passenger work but they came into their own when
employed on mineral trains; during pauses, the boiler
capacity enabled a vast head of steam to be stored so
that a spirited re-start became a feature of the class.
No 1275 was withdrawn from service in the early
twenties and re-appeared for the Stockton and
Darlington Centenary in 1925; the deep and shapely
buffer beam was provided to enable Chaldron wagons,
with non-standard buffers, to be shunted. The
locomotive is now turned out in the attractive livery of
light and dark green with black bands.

19

20

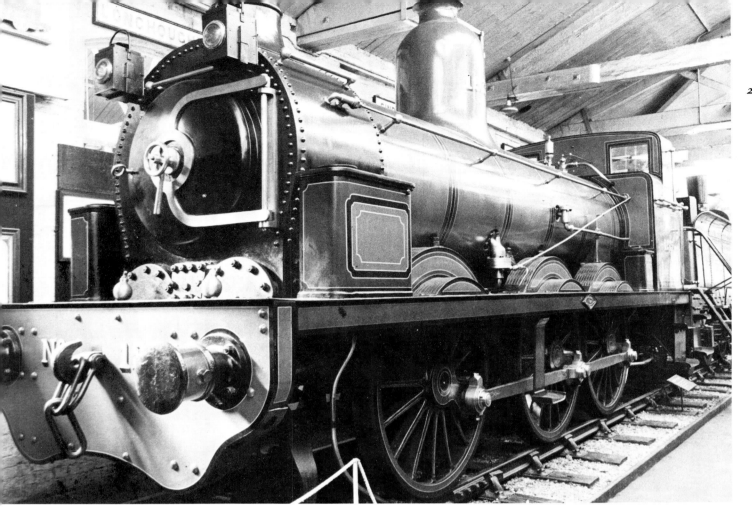

27 When the Grand Junction Railway moved it's works from Edgehill to Crewe the first locomotive to be produced at the new location in 1845 was this 2-2-2 No 49 Columbine. The design was probably originated by Alexander Allan, though it is credited to Francis, son of Richard, Trevithick whose shapely treatment of the smokebox and cylinders set a style which was to be widely followed in later years. The same designer was not responsible for the cab which was a later addition, but its lines do echo the strong verticals of the chimney with geometrical contrast provided by the 6ft driving wheels and slotted splashers. The 2-2-2 became the standard passenger locomotive of the London and North Western Railway, over 150 being built, and 60 of the class were still in service at the turn of the century.

28 The nameplate Yorkshire is from locomotive No 62700 of Gresley's D-49 class introduced in 1927, and North Eastern from A1 class No 60147.

29 Edward Fletcher was one of the pioneers of the steam
30 locomotive, having been apprenticed to the great
31 George Stephenson and, incidentally, involved in the pre-Rainhill tests of the immortal Rocket. After appointment to the position of locomotive superintendent of the North Eastern Railway in 1854, Fletcher was responsible for many successful locomotive designs and he reached his zenith with the introduction of his 901 2-4-0 class at the Gateshead Works. These engines, with their 7ft driving wheels, ornate livery and brasswork and crisp, workmanlike appearance hauled the York-Edinburgh expresses along the East Coast route at speeds up to 70mph and were very popular machines with drivers and firemen alike. No 910, built in 1875 was to complete 50 years in service and when it appeared at the Stockton and Darlington Centenary in 1925 this could have been the occasion on which it made its final bow. With its splendid original livery fully restored and brass burnished, it has stood at York as a monument to an age of pride.

32 Unique among its neighbours at York is the 0-4-2
33 Gladstone resplendent in the golden ochre of the
34 London Brighton and South Coast Railway. No 214, built at Brighton works in 1882, was the first of the class of William Stroudley's largest express passenger locomotives which eventually totalled 36, numbered 172-200 and 214-220, all named. With 6ft 6in diameter driving wheels and no bogie to 'lead' them, the design raised many an eyebrow when if first appeared but the critics were confounded and the locomotives proved to be steady riders and fast and reliable runners with a surprising output of power. With the vast number of standard-gauge locomotives currently preserved by societies and individuals one may wonder where the movement had its beginnings; it was in 1927 that Gladstone was the first to be saved from the scrapyard and near the locomotive stood a plaque bearing the inscription "Preserved in 1927 by the Stephenson Locomotive Society and presented in their Golden Jubilee Year 1959 to the British Transport Commission".
On the wall nearby was displayed a pattern used for forming the mould in which locomotive wheels are cast.

35 In 1884/1885 the locomotive department at the
36 Darlington works of the North Eastern Railway was
37 undergoing a change of leadership; McDonnell had resigned and Worsdell had not yet taken over so, when the production of a new 2-4-0 express passenger locomotive was mooted, the design was formulated by a committee under the presidency of Henry Tennant, the general manager. Worsdell may have arrived on the scene in time to be involved in the final detailing but the fact that the class became known as the Tennant class indicates where credit for the design should lie. While lacking the visual trademarks of any individual designer, these locomotives were regularly employed on the Newcastle-Edinburgh route, at that time the longest non-stop run in Europe, where their speed and economy earned them a popularity with both passengers and staff. No 1463, the first of the class, was built in 1885 and finally withdrawn from service in 1927.

27

28

36

37

38
39
Another 'first' in the North Eastern Railway saga is the 4-4-0 No 1621. On hearing that M class locomotives like this one acquired the nickname of 'Rail Crushers', one could guess that there must be something significant about their weight; in fact, these were the heaviest express passenger locomotives in the country at the time, engine and tender tipping the scales at over 93 tons. No 1621 was the second engine of the class and, together with the first, No 1620, put in some remarkable runs in the 1895 Railway Race to the North; 80½ miles from York to Newcastle in 79 minutes, 124½ miles from Newcastle to Edinburgh in 113 minutes—the figures tell their own story. Designed by Wilson Worsdell and built at Gateshead in 1893, the class eventually numbered nineteen; No 1621 of the NER retained the same number in the LNER after the Grouping in 1924 and actually remained in service until the end of World War II.

40
41
With the undoubted success of the Stirling Eight-Foot Single came demands for bigger and better coaching stock and, as four-wheelers gave way to bogie coaches and weights increased, the limitations of the large single drivers became apparent. Patrick Stirling never retired and died at the age of 75; he was replaced at Doncaster by H. A. Ivatt who, faced with the problem of producing a new express passenger locomotive for the Great Northern Railway, decided upon a 4-4-2 wheel arrangement, an Atlantic. Ivatt had discussed the project with his friend John Aspinall of the Lancashire and Yorkshire Railway Works at Horwich who was similarly inclined and a great rivalry developed as to who would produce the first British 4-4-2. The 'race' ended in June 1898

when out of the Doncaster works rolled No 990, hailed by the press as "the largest and heaviest express engine in the Kingdom". The locomotive was later named after the general manager of the company Henry Oakley and remained the only GNR locomotive to carry a name until 1922 when No 1470 A1 class Pacific Great Northern appeared. The new Atlantics, 21 were built altogether, lived up to their expectations and more, but were soon to be overshadowed by their even more illustrious successors.

42
43
44
45
Although Ivatt was extremely pleased with the success of his Atlantics, he knew that the design was capable of development; for purposes of evaluation, he built a small Atlantic, No 271, with four cylinders driving the leading coupled axle but found only a marginal improvement in performance. Then, in 1902, to the frames, motion and wheels of a 990 he added a boiler of 10in greater diameter and an extended smokebox with a spark arrester and a wide firebox. The result, No 251, was an express locomotive of powerful proportions and astounding performance; the class eventually numbered eighty and between them carried the brunt of the traffic between York and London for 20 years. Ivatt retired in 1911 and his place was taken by a Mr Gresley from the Doncaster Carriage and Wagon Shop; it was he who was later responsible for superheating the 251 class and fitting slightly larger cylinders, thus producing the ultimate in Atlantic development and performance. Even after Gresley introduced his Pacifics in 1922 an Atlantic was often called in to deputise and, while happy to keep to Pacific timings, was occasionally known to improve upon them.

Plate 3
Above left: GNR 4-4-2 No 990
Left: S&D Compo Coach
Above: LBSCR 0-4-2 No 214

SCIENCE MUSEUM

Plate 4
Above: The Agenoria—*York*
Above right: EE Deltic
Right: Rocket (*Replica*)

38

39

42

43

SCIENCE MUSEUM

46 *The first true rail-way company in the world, ie the first body incorporated by Act of Parliament and regulated by the Board of Trade for the conveyance of passengers and freight along a rail road on a commercial basis, was the Stockton and Darlington Railway. At the beginning, the motive power was the horse—the application of steam power for the purpose of locomotion had not yet been proved either necessary or practical; nor was the thought of a 'train' considered a possibility—it was strictly 'one horse, one vehicle'. Well, as we all know, attitudes did change but before then a most famous coach, named* Experiment *was to become a familiar sight as it made its two hour journey between Stockton and Darlington. On this beautiful model, with correct flanged wheels, one can see how passengers were carried outside and in (with, incidentally, a baggage allowance of 14lb and a surcharge of 2d per stone) to a timetable of return trips on Monday, Wednesday, Thursday and Friday and a single journey on Tuesday and Saturday.*

47 *Locomotive models include Stanier Pacific No 6200*
48 *The Princess Royal, the 4-6-0 King George V of the Great Western Railway and a large boilered Atlantic No 1442 of the Great Northern Railway.*

49 Puffing Billy *is assured of a place in history as the*
50 *first steam locomotive to prove successfully that smooth wheels running on a smooth rail were a practical proposition. After earlier efforts which depended on a toothed wheel engaging in a rack, as in the Blenkinsop exhibit at York, the four-coupled* Puffing Billy *appeared in 1814 at Wylam Colliery to designs by William Hedley. It seems that, in his eagerness to demonstrate the tractive effort of his machine, even Hedley had under-estimated the adhesion of four coupled wheels for, after trials in which the cast iron rails were found to be inadequate to take the pounding they received, he rebuilt his locomotive as an*

0-8-0. This spread the load and improved the traction but in 1830, when wrought iron edging was applied to the rails, Hedley found that a return to the 0-4-0 design could be made without any ill-effect and that is the form in which Puffing Billy *has survived. Two vertical cylinders drive, through a fascination of overhead rods and links, a train of gears beneath the chassis which connect to each axle. The locomotive features a return-flue type of boiler which dictates that the firehole is at the same end as the chimney, each located off-centre; the tender was therefore pushed ahead of the engine and, while the fireman worked on a platform between the two, the driver performed his duty from a position to the rear of the bulbous boiler.*

51 *A further locomotive embodying the return-flue type*
52 *of boiler is* Sans Pareil *of 1829 built to the design of Timothy Hackworth. One of the railway pioneers, Hackworth worked for George Stephenson at the Forth Street Works, Newcastle-upon-Tyne and it is to him that the concept of the coupling of driving wheels by rods, as opposed to the gears used hitherto, is accredited. A lay preacher in his off-duty hours, and a man of bold convictions, his experience at the works was wide and varied and, when he heard about the Rainhill Trials, Hackworth decided to enter a locomotive of his own design. He knew that one of his competitors was to be Robert Stephenson with an 0-2-2 entry but, working mostly in his spare time and at his own expense, he went ahead with the construction of his own entry at the Shildon Works of the Stockton and Darlington Railway. In the event, however,* Sans Pareil *was found to be slightly overweight for the rules of the competition and, even in the running trials, encountered trouble with the boiler feed pump and shortage of water; the locomotive failed to complete the course and therefore retired to be subsequently employed at various Lancashire collieries before being preserved for posterity.*

46

47

48

LOCOMOTIVES (1891-1911)

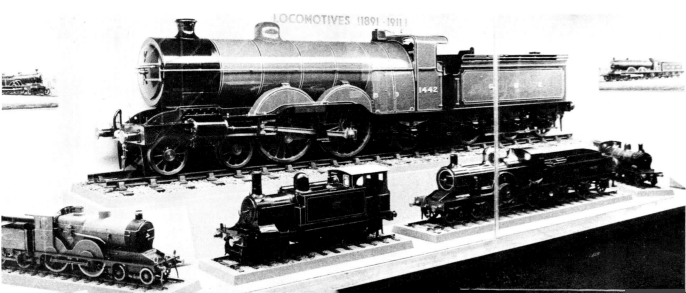

51
52

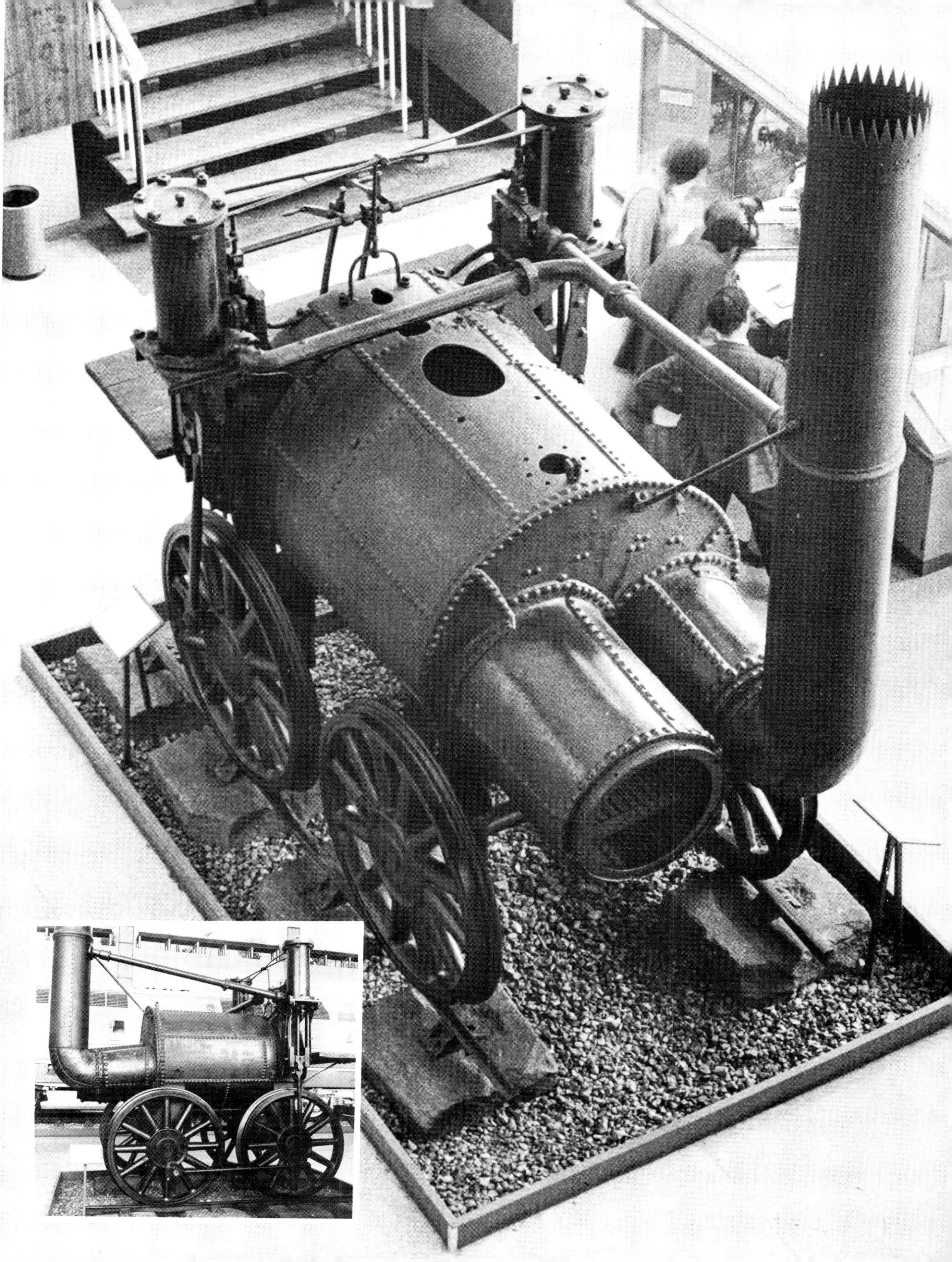

53   The Rainhill Competition itself was the outcome of
54   disagreement between the directors of the newly-formed
55   Liverpool and Manchester Railway as to the most
suitable source of motive power to adopt. Some
favoured steam, others advocated cables while the
remainder could see no alternative to the horse, so to
settle the matter it was decided to evaluate the potential
of the steam locomotive in a competition; the rules
included a requirement for the locomotive to "consume
its own smoke", to cost not more than £500, to be
within certain weight limitations and to haul a
specified load depending upon those limitations. Of the
five entrants Perseverance and Cyclopede were, at
6mph too slow; Novelty with its mechanically operated
fire-drawing bellows giving constant trouble, had to
retire despite some amazing sprints of up to 40mph.
The fate of Sans Pareil has already been described
and so the undisputed winner was the immortal
Rocket, weighing $4\frac{1}{2}$ tons and hauling its $12\frac{1}{2}$ ton
load over the $1\frac{1}{2}$ mile test course at an average speed of
15 mph for ten consecutive return trips.
The prize went to this product of the genius of
Robert Stephenson and the pattern was set for the
development of the greatest transport revolution the
world had ever known—the steam railway. For two
features of Rocket were to become standard practice
on every steam locomotive that ever went into service;
the tubed boiler which enabled the gases from the fire to
be more efficiently applied to heating the water than
the single flue, and the discharge of the cylinder
exhaust up the chimney in such a way that the fire is
drawn through the tubes instead of rising by
convection. These features can clearly be seen in the
full-size replica. Although Rocket now exists in a
more modified, and denuded, condition than in the
Rainhill days, the simple nameplate is carried with
pride and, as she stands dwarfed by her mighty

descendants, one wonders how Stephenson would have
felt about the way it has all turned out.

56   This full-size model of Rocket is cut-away on one
side so that the interior details of boiler, smokebox
and cylinders can be inspected; the cylinders, by the
way, are positioned as they were when the loco was
first built—later modification set them at a lower angle.

57   It was the world of industry that was the first to
58   recognise the advantages of the 'rail-way', to use men
to push loaded wagons and later to use horses to haul
them; then, at colliery and mine, stationary steam
engines used cables to move the trains and then the
idea of using a smaller mobile engine as a
self-powered entity became a reality. While industry
handed down the principle to the outside world,
industry itself was able to become more productive as
both time and manpower were saved by the employment
of the steam locomotive; the revolution gained
momentum as machine took over from man and the
industrial locomotive developed as a strain apart from
its main line cousins. Invariably small in stature and
produced in 'one-offs' or very nominal runs. these
fussy little fellows became the moving spirit behind the
industrial expansion of the age and their hardy
heritage kept them going, often with only the
minimum of maintenance. It is in recognition of a
history of uncomplaining service by such as these that
this 0-4-0ST humbly stands today in very
distinguished company indeed. Bauxite No 2, built in
1874 by Black Hawthorn, was thus named, naturally,
by the British Aluminium Co who were the first
owners; in 1947 the locomotive was presented by ICI
to the North East Historical and Industrial
Locomotive Society from where it was selected to
represent its line at the Science Museum.

57

58

59
60
61 The Castles of the Great Western Railway have been hailed as the most successful locomotives ever to run in Great Britain and, while many would challenge such a claim, there is no escaping the fact that their performance figures do indicate a high degree of efficiency. C. B. Collett, who succeeded Churchward as chief mechanical engineer at Swindon, developed the Star class by fitting a larger boiler and cylinders of 1in greater diameter and produced Caerphilly Castle No 4073, the first of a total of 171 Castles which were to appear. It is fitting that this particular locomotive, as the first of the class, should be preserved; being built in 1923 it was put on show at the Wembley Exhibition of 1925. Production continued until interrupted by the outbreak of World War II and after the cessation of hostilities many more were turned out with the only minor difference of an improved superheater; that this should be the sole modification possible after over 20 years of service is itself a tribute to the basic soundness of the design. The Castles produced some notable runs on the West of England expresses, particularly the 'Cornish Riviera Express' and the 'Cheltenham Flyer'; on the latter, more correctly the 'Cheltenham Spa Express', an average speed of over 80mph for the 77½ mile journey from Swindon to Paddington was recorded in June 1932.

62
63 The prototype Deltic Diesel in its dramatic light blue livery was presented to the Science Museum by the makers, Napier and English Electric in 1959. Built in 1955 it ran on trials in the London Midland Region although it was never taken on to BR inventory, and it differs from the stud of 22 locomotives subsequently supplied for use on the East Coast main line only in detail. The name is derived from the engine layout, in section the shape of a triangle or delta, and two 18-cylinder engines supply electric power to six traction motors to provide a total of 3,300hp making it the most powerful single unit diesel electric locomotive in the world. Changeover switches permit the locomotive to be run on just one engine if required for slow running or in emergency, and a complete engine change can be carried out through removable roof panels in about eight hours. Sustained running at high speed makes this locomotive a remarkable performer and the 22 Deltics now do the work of 55 Pacifics; steam enthusiasts may question that rate of exchange but it is a cold, economic fact of railway operation.

59

60
61

RAILWAY HAND SIGNAL LAMP (1868)

This is a one-handed railway signal lamp patented in 1868 by Messrs. Brown & Jones. The casing is cylindrical, and has at the back a colza lamp with a concave reflector, and a flat glass in the door at the front. Between the oil lamp and the glass are three hinged "spectacle" frames connected to press knobs at the top, by depressing which, either of the coloured glasses fitted can be placed before the flame. The knobs are moved by the thumb, and springs are added, which, when a trigger at the top is released, cause the glasses to swing upwards into the top portion of the casing.

Presented by J. Cowdy & Co., London.

Inv. 1871-35

Plate 5
Above left: Caerphilly Castle
Left: Caerphilly Castle
Above: Hand Signal Lamp

LEICESTER

Plate 6
Above: MR 4-2-2 No 118
Above right: Midland Montage
Right: MR 2-4-0 No 158A

LEICESTER

64
65
66
A challenger for the title of the longest serving preserved locomotive must surely be the 2-4-0 No 158A of the Midland Railway; this veteran was built at the Derby Works in 1866 as one of a class of 29 no-nonsense workhorses designed by Matthew Kirtley, a practical engineer in every sense of the word. Typically mid-Victorian in appearance with curved running plate and outside springing, the 156 class proved excellent performers and, when the call for greater power went out, it was the robust construction of the class which enabled the cylinder size to be increased on two separate occasions. The preserved specimen was renumbered MR No 2 in 1907 and retained the same number at the Grouping but became LMS No 20002 in 1934; throughout the war the locomotive served in black livery and went on running until immediately prior to Nationalisation when withdrawal came after an unbroken service of 81 years. Restoration was carried out at Derby when the original number was re-instated and the locomotive was painted in the manner for which the Midland Railway became famous—two coats of lead grey paint, four of purple brown, a top coat of crimson lake with purple brown mixed into it and finished off with five coats of varnish.

67
68
69
The main reason that the large single-drivers faded from fashion was the lack of adhesion when starting with a heavy train; once they were on the move they were long-striding free-runners with the added advantage of simplicity in construction and maintenance—after all, the large wheel needed fewer rpm, therefore it turned more slowly and the internal mechanics had a longer life. It was therefore a happy day when Mr Holt came up with a device to counter this slipping tendency, namely his steam operated sanding gear, for it enabled the railway operator to re-introduce the single-driver with all its attractive features. The Midland Railway was among those to do so and, for this purpose, Samuel Waite Johnson turned out a fine 4-2-2 locomotive from the Derby Works in 1887; ninety-five of these were produced over a 13 year period and their well proportioned appearance was set off handsomely by the unique flared chimney. One of the class, No 117, was the joint holder of the 19th century steam speed record at 90mph and another, No. 129,

once hurried a 325 ton train the 51½ miles from Kettering to Northampton in 59 minutes. The preserved No 118 was built in 1897, renumbered 673 in 1907 and Grouped into the LMS as No 673; fittingly, it was the last of the 'Johnson Spinners', as the class became known, to remain in service and was withdrawn in 1928.

70
Preserved electric locomotives are few and far between and one particularly significant example in the North Eastern Railway is Bo-Bo No 1. One section of the docks railway at Newcastle-on-Tyne opened in 1870 was, of necessity, sharply curved and heavily graded—not a happy prospect for steam operation—and when other electrification work was taking place locally in 1904, it was decided to include this branch also. Two locomotives were ordered from the Brush Company of Leicestershire to work on 600 volts dc and they continued in operation there for sixty years until being replaced by diesels. Both locomotives carried alternative current pick-up systems for either third-rail or overhead operation. NER No 1 built in 1902 became No 6480 in 1946 and BR No 26500 in 1948; present livery is apple green with black bands and white edging and, in addition to the NER crest, the BR lion and wheel emblem also appears with the BR number.

71
The 0-4-0 saddle tank locomotive was built in Leicestershire in 1906 and after a nomadic existence of 60 years has now returned to the place of its birth to be placed on permanent exhibition. The Brush Electrical Engineering Company was not one of the major constructors of steam locomotives, but the firm did supply equipment to steam tramways in many parts of Europe before passing on to the production of electrical tramway equipment; however, one of the last steam locomotives they built was to Works No 314 supplied to work at Swansea Harbour. The engine was later acquired by the Great Western Railway and numbered 921 but in 1928 it moved to Eynsham, Oxon, and then in 1931 to an oil refinery in North Kent—at the latter location, not surprisingly, it was converted to oil-burning and in that form it was presented to the Museum in 1967.

BIRMINGHAM

72　In sharp contrast to the massive Pacific standing
73　nearby, the two narrow gauge 0-4-0 saddle tank
74　locomotives are exhibits of absorbing interest and
enable striking comparisons to be made with their
main-line cousin.

Leonard, *built in 1919 with the more conventional
round-topped saddle tank, features wheels and valve
gear of almost model-like proportions. The locomotive
is one of six survivors of a class built by Bagnall and
Sons between 1897 and 1919, the others being named*
Isabel, Peter, Lady Luxborough, Pixie, *and*
Wendy, *and carried the Works No 2087. The gauge
is 2ft.*

*Of similar gauge is the Kerr-Stuart example,
identified by the flat-topped saddle tank of greater
capacity, built to Works No 4250 in 1922 and
named* Lorna Doone. *This locomotive is fitted with
a coal bunker on either side of the firebox, each one
about the size of a medium suitcase, and was
previously in service with the Devon County Council
on road construction projects; the lower plate on the
bunker side carried the words "R. M. Stone County
Surveyor Barnstaple". Four other examples of the
class survive, one is un-named but the others are*
Stanhope, Pixie *and* Peter Pan—*the works of
James Barrie must have been very widely read in the
narrow-gauge world.*

75　In 1937 the London Midland and Scottish Railway
76　introduced a prestige express passenger train on to
77　their West Coast route between London and

*Glasgow and, in recognition of the Royal event of that
year, entitled it 'The Coronation Scot'. The
locomotives were to the striking new Pacific design of
William Stanier and they caused quite a stir when
they appeared in their sleek blue streamlined casings
with silver styling flashes and matching coaches; five in
number they carried Royal names and their tight
scheduling of London to Glasgow in 6½ hours and their
performance were well matched. In 1938 ten more
were built and named after Duchesses; all were
turned out in LMS red livery, five streamlined with
gold flashes and five non-streamlined, and these were
followed by 21 further examples built during the war;
the first of this later batch, streamlined red and gold,
was No 6235 named* City of Birmingham.

*Because of the war, the gorgeous livery was not renewed
and, indeed, even the streamlined casings themselves
were removed after the war to facilitate maintenance;
this removal, incidentally, left a distinctive chamfer on
the smokebox top forward of the chimney, but the
original profile was restored as the locomotives were
called into the shops. To complete the story, two more
examples of the class appeared with modifications by
H. G. Ivatt making 38 in all; LMS No 6235 was
built in 1939, de-streamlined in 1946, became BR No
46235 at Nationalisation and now stands in the livery
in which she ran until withdrawal in 1964. A novel
feature of the present method of display is that the
locomotive can be moved by electrical power along a
short length of track to the accompaniment of a tape
recording of chimney blasts.*

72

73

75

76

SWINDON

78 *In the entrance porch at the Swindon Museum hangs a Royal Train crest, together with the most appropriate name and numberplate from the last of Mr Collett's outstandingly successful 4-cylinder express passenger Castle class. Production of the class continued right up until 1950, three years after Nationalisation, by which time no fewer than 165 had been turned out. By comparison, the larger and more powerful King class which followed was limited to a run of 30 engines built between 1927 and 1930.*
The plaque, inscribed with the names of the chairman of the Western Area Board of the British Transport Commission and the Mayor of Swindon commemmorates the opening of the Museum in June 1962.

79 *The broad gauge Firefly class was the first locomotive type to be produced in any quantity for the Great Western Railway and a remarkable 62 were built between 1840 and 1842. Based largely on the North Star design, but with many improvements incorporated by Daniel Gooch, such as the enlarged boiler and firebox, the class soon distinguished itself as the fastest in the country at the time. Indeed, on the occasion of the opening of the London to Exeter line in 1844 one of the class,* Actaeon *by name, made the entire return journey at an average speed of 41½mph. Another example is here perpetuated by this silver-plated model, the name* Victoria *accounting for the regal embellishments; while certain discrepancies between the model and the real thing may be detected, they exist for purely practical reasons. This model is in fact a coffee urn and spent many years dispensing the beverage in the Refreshment Room of Swindon Station to the fortification of the early traveller but not, it is recorded, to the satisfaction of Mr Brunel.*

80 *Among the smaller exhibits can be found this working model of a signal gantry constructed entirely in brass; it has been left unpainted so that the finest detail and expert workmanship can be fully appreciated.*

81 *Over the buffer beam of the Dean Goods can be seen the headboard of the titled train 'The Merchant Venturer'. Under its former title of 'The Bristolian' the train was introduced in 1935 between Paddington and Bristol to mark the centenary of the opening of that line and, as such, it ran until the outbreak of World War II. Subsequent trains running the same route were later to assume the same title and then to mark the Festival of Britain in 1951 'The Merchant Venturer', named in recognition of the trading heritage of the port of Bristol, was born; it departed from Paddington at 11.15am and on the return left Bristol at 4.35pm but, with its intermediate calls, it was a slower train than its non-stop predecessor.*

82 *A decorative fret bearing an elaboration of the Somerset and Dorset Railway monogram hangs above the nameplate of the Churchward 4-cylinder Star class locomotive No 4057* Princess Elizabeth. *This nameplate carries the crest of the GWR, the arms of London and Bristol, and an inscription which reads, "H.R.H. The Princess Elizabeth drove this engine from the erecting shop to the Station at Swindon on 15th November 1950".*
The large photograph depicts the broad gauge Lord of the Isles *of the Gooch Iron Duke class of 1847. This locomotive was withdrawn from service in 1884 and preserved at Swindon but was regrettably scrapped in 1906; the driving wheels, however, were retained and can be seen to the right of the picture.*

78

63

BIRMINGHAM

Plate 7
Above left: City of Birmingham
Left: City of Birmingham
Above: Signals at Swindon

SWINDON

Plate 8
Above: Lode Star
Above right: North Star
Right: Dean Goods

83 Brunel is acknowledged here by this vast mural of the old engraving showing the imposing western portal of his Box Tunnel between Bath and Chippenham. This tunnel runs dead straight for two miles and boasts a remarkable curiosity; built on a climbing gradient of 1 in 100 from west to east it is so orientated that on a certain date once a year the rising sun shines directly down the bore and can be seen from the western end. The phenomenon occurs every 9th of April—Brunel's birthday. It is difficult to accept this as coincidence yet, at the same time, one cannot imagine Brunel engineering his approaches at either end of the tunnel solely in order to obtain this precise alignment. It is an interesting reflection that, in the days of steam, residual smoke inside the tunnel would have prevented direct vision from one end to the other and so whether the bore was placed thus by accident or by design will have to remain a mystery. The figure on the left is a railway 'policeman' with arm outstretched giving the 'line clear' indication to the broad gauge locomotive just emerging from the tunnel mouth. He stands by a signal post carrying the arrow head of the Fantail type of signal; clear of visual distraction at the top of the post would be found a 'disc and crossbar' indicator.

The nameplate Viscount Horne is from the Castle class 4-6-0 locomotive No 5086 while the adjacent numberplate No 5048 is from a similar locomotive originally named Cranbrook Castle and later Earl of Devon.

84 Viewed from the Gooch Gallery, the three tender locomotives appear to be arranged in echelon but in fact their rear buffers are exactly in line. The nameplate on the far wall G. J. Churchward is from Castle No 7017; the great man would probably have had mixed feelings had he known that his name was to appear in full George Jackson Churchward on a later locomotive—BR Brush Type 4 Diesel No D1664.

85 Behind the original 8ft driving wheels from Daniel
86 Gooch's 4-2-2 Lord of the Isles and on the same
87 length of broad gauge track stands the replica of North Star; it had to be a replica because the original engine, withdrawn from service in 1870, met its end in the grand clear-out at Swindon in 1906.

Built by Robert Stephenson & Co of Newcastle for the 5ft 6in gauge New Orleans Railway in America, the locomotive was shipped to the States but, due to some business difficulty, was not delivered and therefore returned to Britain where it was converted to the 7ft gauge for the GWR. On 31st May 1838, a director's special, the first passenger train on the Great Western Railway, ran from Paddington to Maidenhead; at the head was the newly named North Star, an outstanding performer compared with other GWR locomotives. A further 11 of the same type followed and were named Dog Star, Evening Star Lode Star, Morning Star, Polar Star, Red Star Rising Star, Royal Star, Shooting Star, Western Star and Bright Star; all but the last of these names were to re-appear on Churchward's 4-6-0 Star class of the early 1900s. The replica was built at Swindon using such original components as had survived, being completed in 1925 in time to be put on display at the Stockton and Darlington Centenary Exhibition of that year; as the sole full-size example of the broad gauge locomotive, it comes as quite a surprise to the visitor to see just how far apart those wheels really are.

88 Wearing a 'light engine' headcode, No 2516 is the
89 proud survivor of a class of locomotive which in its
90 day could be found almost anywhere on the Great Western doing almost anything. Designed by William Dean and built between 1883 and 1898, the 2301 class eventually numbered 280, an outstanding production bearing in mind that it was the first Great Western locomotive to incorporate a chassis with inside frames where previously the decorative outside frames had been employed. Intended as a freight engine but inevitably used on local passenger and branch lines, the class was later superheated which gave it a new lease of life; indeed, some rendered a service life of around the 60 year mark. The Dean Goods, as the class was known, led a routine and unglamorous life (including war service overseas) and it is satisfying to know that this humble existence has been rewarded by a place in a museum. This representative example, No 2516, was built in 1897, fitted with a Belpaire firebox in 1913, superheated in 1935 and was withdrawn from service in 1956

83

84

86

NORTH STAR (REPLICA)

87

91 *Descended from the 4-4-0* Duke of Cornwall *via*
92 *the Bulldog, Badminton and Athara classes, the Cities*
93 *comprised ten locomotives numbered from 3710 to
3719. Basically a design by William Dean, the class
was built in 1903 with a Churchward-modified front
end and No 4 Standard Boiler, and soon proved to
be a match for the tight schedules of the west of
England passenger expresses.* City of Truro, *No
3717, was the 2,000th engine to be built at Swindon
and achieved fame on 9th May 1904 when, hauling
the Ocean Mail from Plymouth to Paddington, it was
reported to have reached a speed of just over 100mph,
the first British locomotive to do so, down Wellington
Bank. Accurate records of the run were never
available and so the claim must remain open to doubt,
but the class went on to make a good account of itself.
In 1931* City of Truro *was withdrawn from service
and placed on display in the York Museum but in
1957 it was restored to its former GWR glory with
lake coloured frames and monogrammed tender and,
carrying its original number 3440, put to work on
light scheduled trains between Didcot and
Southampton, with the occasional appearance on
enthusiasts specials up and down the country. Final
retirement and restoration to later livery and numbering
came in 1963 and it is now its own memorial to a
long and illustrious career.*

94 *Churchward's quest for an improved breed of*
95 *locomotive led him to evaluate American practice and
to purchase three French four-cylinder compound
Atlantics, No 102* La France, *No 103* President
and No 104 Alliance. *The result of his study
appeared in 1906 and was a four-cylinder simple
Atlantic 4-4-2 to be named* North Star *in
acknowledgement of the start of things way back in
1837. After three years service No 40 was converted
to a 4-6-0 and renumbered No 4000, to conform with*

*others of the class which had already been built, and
the Star was born; the production run continued until
the outbreak of World War I by which time 73 of
the class had been built. The naming style began with
Stars, through Knights and Kings (changed to
Monarchs in 1927 with the introduction of the King
class) on to Queens, Princes and Princesses and
finally Abbeys.* Lode Star *No 4003 was one of the
first constructed, entering service in 1907; scrapping
began in 1934 and, while others of the class were
converted to Castles,* Lode Star *survived in original
form until being withdrawn in 1951. It was no doubt
due to the success of the Stars that Churchward
favoured the development of the four-cylinder 4-6-0 for
express passenger duties on the Great Western and,
although he did build a long-boilered Star with a 4-6-2
wheel arrangement (*The Great Bear, *Britain's first
Pacific locomotive) it was the old formula which was
later to produce the legendary Castles and Kings.*

96 *Regarded by many as the last true Great Western*
97 *locomotives to be built, the 94XX 0-6-0 pannier tanks
are here represented by the sturdy leader of the class
No 9400. Designed by F. W. Hawksworth, the ten
originals were constructed at Swindon in 1947 and a
further 200 followed after Nationalisation; duties
included local freight, heavy shunting and passenger
working, and seven of the later examples were
stationed at Bromsgrove on the old LMS line and
used for banking on the Lickey Incline. The water
tanks are the largest ever fitted to Great Western
0-6-0 panniers and hold 1,300 gallons, while the
bunker can carry 3½ tons of coal; ready for the road
the complete locomotive weighs 55 tons. No 9400 was
withdrawn from service in 1959 and restored properly
to its original livery; it writes the final chapter in the
110 year history of the Great Western Railway
Locomotive.*

91

92

94

95

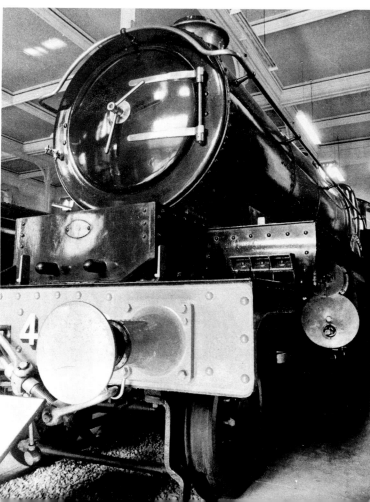

VISITORS ARE NOT ALLOWED ON THIS LOCOMOTIVE

9400

9400

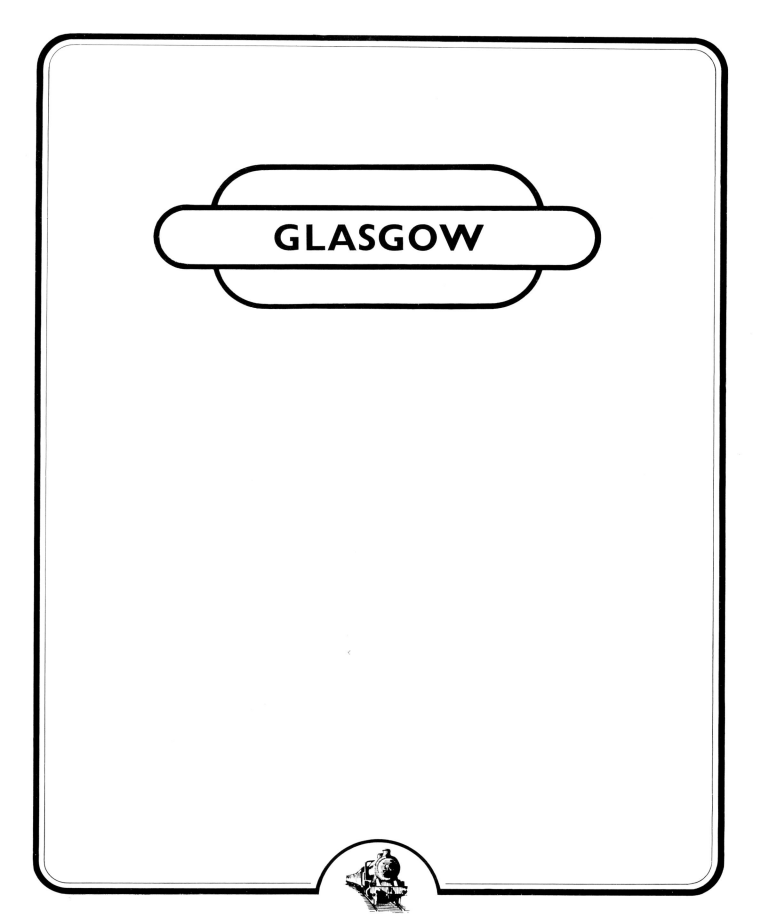

GLASGOW

98 With a fanfare of polished brass numberplates, the
99 crystallisation of the Scottish Railway system is
100 recalled by the famous names of the big five
101 companies, namely The Highland, the Great North
102 of Scotland, the Caledonian, the North British and,
103 not illustrated, the Glasgow and South Western. In
the 19th century, Scottish railway companies
numbered a phenomenal 212 but some never got
beyond the horse-drawn stage, others failed and faded
while quite a few were simply abandoned; it was the
survival of the fittest that enabled the whole thing to
be rationalised into the five major companies which
were incorporated in the mid-1840s. At the 1925
Grouping the LNER absorbed the North British and
the Great North of Scotland while the Highland, the
Caledonian and the Glasgow and South Western went
into the LMS.

104 The celebrated Caledonian Single 4-2-2 locomotive is
105 an isolated 'one-off' example which has happily
106 survived since being built by Nielson & Co, in
107 Glasgow in 1886. Placed on display at the
Edinburgh Exhibition of that year, No 123 tended
not to be taken too seriously as a challenger for the
powerful 4-4-0s at that time hauling the main-line
passenger expresses over the testing gradients of the

Caledonian Railway. But when put to work, the 7ft
single caused nothing less than a sensation and, with its
long striding gait, seemed to be ideally geared for
gradient and flat alike; in the Race to Edinburgh in
1888, heading the Carlisle to Edinburgh train, the
$100\frac{3}{4}$ miles were covered in $107\frac{3}{4}$ minutes and this,
let it be remembered, over the 8 mile Beattock Bank.
As passenger stock became heavier and trains longer,
the single-wheeler, lacking adhesion for starting, faded
from fashion and No 123 became the prestige CR
locomotive hauling director's specials; it was
renumbered in 1914 and became 1123. At the 1924
Grouping, the Caledonian Railway was absorbed into
the LMS so this leisurely life of grace ended and, now
numbered 14010, this unique locomotive was returned
to normal working on local trains, mainly on the
Tayside route between Perth and Dundee. There she
became the last single-wheeler in use anywhere in
Britain and was finally withdrawn and set aside for
preservation in 1935. However, after a complete
overhaul and restoration to Caledonian livery—and the
original number—No 123 was given a further lease
of life in 1958 and was thereafter much in evidence
hauling enthusiasts' specials in all parts of Britain;
ultimate retirement followed all too soon.

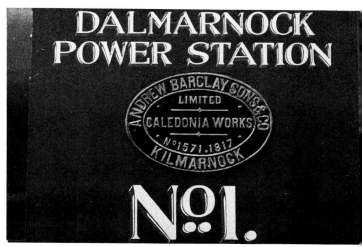

SWINDON

Plate 9
Above left: City of Truro
Left: 0-6-0PT No 9400
Above: Pristine Paintwork

GLASGOW

Plate 10
Above: Platform Trolley
Above right: CR 0-6-0 No 828
Right: CR 0-6-0 No 828

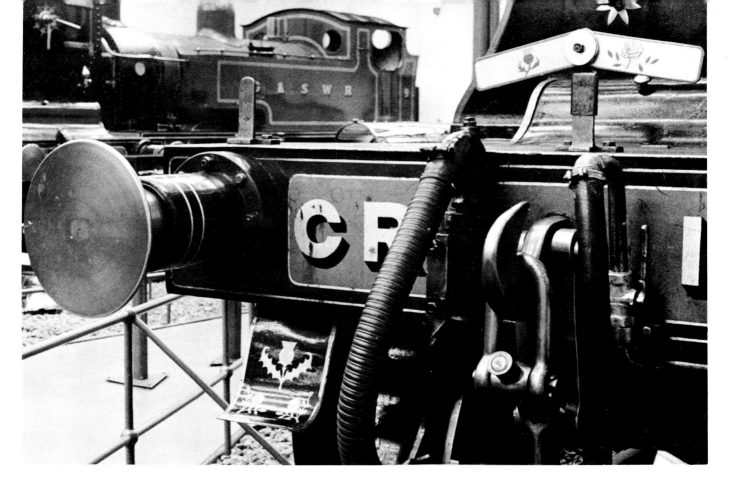

108 From Inverness, the Highland Railway ran east to
109 Elgin, south to Perth, west to Kyle of Lochalsh and
north to Thurso and, faced with severe gradients and
tight curves, David Jones as locomotive
superintendent had to produce locomotives which were
powerful yet small. In 1874, with his 4-4-0 F class,
he turned out one of the heaviest and most powerful
engines in Europe and then, 20 years later,
astonished the locomotive world with the introduction of
the first 4-6-0 locomotive in Britain, with flangeless
centre drivers. This concept was something quite new,
yet so confident of the design was Jones that a
production run of fifteen locomotives was ordered
straight off the drawing board; this confidence was
fully vindicated and what was to become known as the
Jones Goods distinguished itself as one of the most
successful and trouble-free locomotives in the country.
No 103 here was built in 1894 by Sharp, Stewart
& Co, at Glasgow and became LMS No 17916 at
the Grouping; withdrawn from service in 1934 and
earmarked for preservation this eminent locomotive was
overhauled and returned to work on enthusiasts'
specials in 1959, finally to be retired in 1966. The
unique HR livery of Stroudley's 'improved engine
green', whether originally worn by this locomotive or
not, is a perfect blend with the colours of nature to be
found in the Highlands.

110 While this 0-6-0 tender locomotive gives a workmanlike
111 impression, its classical ancestry is apparent in
112 various points of detail such as the neat merging of the
front splasher, sandbox and smokebox wing plate.
Dating from 1899, No 828 was built at the
Caledonian Railway's St Rollox Works to the design
of J. F. McIntosh and was one of the 812 class of 96
trim workhorses intended for main line goods but
eventually employed on mixed traffic anywhere
between Carlisle and Aberdeen; the locomotive was
renumbered LMS No 17566 at the Grouping and,
at Nationalisation, BR No 57566. In 1963 it was
withdrawn from service, purchased by the Scottish
Locomotive Preservation Trust and beautifully
restored to its original Caledonian livery in which it
now stands as the sole survivor of what could be
called the 'McIntosh Standard Goods'. By the tender
stands a relic of the early days of the CR, a horse
breaking cart, while the England and Scotland
nameplates once indicated to travellers that they were
crossing the border on the West Coast main line.

113 Dugald Drummond designed powerful 4-4-0
114 locomotives for the North British Railway, and when
115 these were improved in 1913 by W. P. Reid, the
locomotive superintendent, the result was the
superheated Glen class, 32 untiring locomotives of
massive proportions. Mainly employed on the steeply
graded and torturous route from the Clyde via Fort
William to Mallaig, for which they were ideally
suited, the class was named after glens in the area.
The pity of painted 'names' is that none survive; none,
that is, save Glen Douglas No 256 built at
Cowlairs in 1913 and launched, as she now stands,
resplendent in the autumnal North British livery.
Grouped into the LNER, the locomotive became No
9256 of the D34 class and later, in 1946, No 2469;
Nationalisation brought a final number, BR No
62469, and, while withdrawal came in 1959,
restoration immediately followed and the locomotive
was soon back at work hauling enthusiasts' special
trains. After a strenuous life of over 50 years, No
256 is now in well-earned retirement. Nearby stands
an item of LMS platform equipment used to
dispense warmth and comfort to travellers facing the
Scottish weather, while alongside the bogie lies the
engine and chassis of a steam vehicle unearthed in the
locality. Seated by the tender in bronze is Mr John
Walker, general manager of the North British
Railway from 1874-1901.

116 Standing by a lamp-post from the Edinburgh and
117 Northern Railway (later to be named the Edinburgh,
118 Perth and Dundee Railway before becoming part of
the North British Railway) is the Great North of
Scotland Railway locomotive Gordon Highlander.
No 49 was one of six of the F class engines built by
the NB Locomotive Co in Glasgow in 1920, the
remaining two of the class being built at the GNSR
Works at Inverurie, Aberdeenshire. Together, these
eight 4-4-0 passenger locomotives were the only ones to
be named by the GNSR—all other motive power was
numbered—and they were designed by W. Pickersgill
as a superheated version of his V class of 1909.
With the Grouping, No 49 became LNER No
6849 and, in 1946, 2277 and was to end its days as
BR No 62277; for some time before withdrawal it
was appropriately stationed at Elgin and was the
only survivor of the class still in service. Restored to
GNSR green, though it probably originally appeared
in black, it was given an occasional airing on specials.

108

109

CA
St R

III

II2

117 By Gordon Highlander's tender is an interesting item of platform equipment used at Aberdeen Station when Queen Victoria was pausing en route to and from Balmoral Castle. It is a kitchen trolley used for the conveyance of freshly cooked meals from the hotel to the Royal Train at the station and is equipped with its own spirit warmer. It must be one of the more unique vehicles to bear the coat-of-arms of the Great North of Scotland Railway.

118 The model Viking ship in the foreground is, in fact, a wrought iron weather-vane from the Hawes Pier at South Queensferry. The ferry there used to ply continuously across to North Queensferry in the shadow of the mighty Forth Rail Bridge; ending its days as a BR ferry, the service finally ceased on the opening of the Forth Road Bridge.

119 The Glasgow and South Western Railway, the last of the Scottish 'Big Five' companies, virtually disappeared at the Grouping and, although it was absorbed into the LMS by name, its stock of locomotives became completely liquidated. Therefore, when a G&SWR representative was required for the Museum, it was not a simple matter to trace one; however, as luck would have it, a couple of 0-6-0 tanks were still in existence and it is one of these that now perpetuates the memory of a great railway. In 1917, when the locomotive superintendent was Peter, son of Dugald, Drummond, the G&SWR had three 0-6-0Ts built at the NB Loco Co's Hydepark Works in Glasgow; numbered 5, 7 and 9 they were required for dock shunting duties. No 9 was thus employed at Greenock, was renumbered 324 in 1919 and, at The Grouping, became LMS No 16379. In 1934 the locomotive was sold to a colliery in Denbeighshire, subsequently passing into NCB ownership and it was from that unlikely location that it was happily acquired and returned to its native Scotland for restoration.

120 Representing a less familiar type of locomotive is No 1571 from the Kilmarnock Works of Andrew Barclay. It began its career at the Irvine Munitions Factory, Ayrshire, in 1918 where there was a clear requirement for a locomotive of the fireless type which produced no flame or sparks; the principle is that a charge of steam is taken on from a remote stationary boiler instead and this is sufficient to keep the locomotive at work for about $2\frac{1}{2}$ hours. In the early twenties No 1571 was acquired by Glasgow Corporation for use at Dalmarnock Power Station where it continued in operation under SSEB ownership; it was presented back to the city again in 1969, restored and repainted.

GLASGOW & S W RLY.
Nº 9
N.B. LOCO Cº 1917

CLAPHAM

121 Conversation pieces from parlour and boardroom
122 included commemorative trowels.

123 The bustle of street traffic in the early days of the
124 railway is admirably captured by these delightful
125 models. As more London terminal stations were
126 built, the transfer of passengers between them must
     have provided a useful increase in passenger loads for
     the operators of the omnibus, who probably regarded
     the appearance of station names among the painted
     advertisements as something of a status symbol.

127 The Victorian music hall was quick to recognise the
128 spicy possibilities of a railway romance; a chance
     encounter between travellers sharing the same
     compartment, and the novel magnetism of a member
     of a train crew each provided song material as these
     colourful examples of contemporary sheet music show.
     The chorus of another favourite ran as follows:
     "Birmingham and Sandringham, Ulverton and
     Wolverton,
     Dorchester and Porchester, Rochester and Ryde,
     Arlington and Darlington, Torrington and
     Warrington,
     She said she'd sure to find it in my Bradshaws Guide."

129 While song sheets are not available at the Museum
     Shop, the establishment does offer the visitor a full
     range of picture postcards, souvenirs and booklets.
     The British Railways standard Class 7 locomotive
     Britannia, numbered 70000 as the first of the class,
     is prominently illustrated behind one of the
     nameplates.

130 From this model of the original Euston Station it
131 can be seen how the mighty Doric Arch instilled
     feelings of stability, security and safety in the
     apprehensive rail traveller of the day. The

commemorative plaque from the famous waiting room
announces that . . .

132 This historic turntable was unearthed at Euston
     during the 1963 rebuilding; it bears the maker's
     name 'C. H. Wild' of London and is dated 1846 but
     it was probably installed at Euston in 1848 when the
     premises were extended. Having a diameter of around
     12ft its operation would be confined to the transfer of
     wagons and coaches from one track to another and it
     gives an indication of the wheelbase of contemporary
     rolling stock.

133 The study of railway heraldry on its own could be the
134 subject of a complete book, so wide and varied were
135 the devices employed to impart corporate identity to a
     railway company. Heraldic conventions were
     frequently swept aside in the design of an imposing
     crest, which grew from an adaptation of the coat-of-
     arms of a local county or city to a gilded expression of
     regal magnificence. The passing of the smaller
     companies into larger groups spelled the decline of this
     colourful period of railway history, the East
     Lancashire Railway, for instance, merged into the
     Lancashire and Yorkshire Railway in 1859, and
     after the great Amalgamation of 1924, only the big
     four companies survived with separate identities.
     Previous associations were sometimes acknowledged, as
     in the case of the LNER adopting the motto of the
     Great Central Railway 'Forward' but since the
     Nationalisation BR crests have shown complete
     impartiality in their make-up. Just as the
     Lancashire and Yorkshire's earlier effort, which
     perhaps overdid the maritime connections, was
     superseded by a more compact and explicit design, so
     the BR crest has distilled through various
     combinations of lions, wheels and crowns to the
     present double arrow symbol.

127
128

129

IT IS THE LARGEST RAILWAY WAITING ROOM
IN THE BRITISH ISLES, MEASURING 126 FEET IN LENGTH, 61 FEET
IN WIDTH AND 64 FEET IN HEIGHT · · · · THE FLAT PANELLED
CEILING IS THE LARGEST OF ITS TYPE IN THE WORLD.
EUSTON STATION, THE FIRST MAIN LINE TERMINUS IN LONDON,
WAS BROUGHT FULLY INTO USE ON
17th SEPTEMBER 1838.

Plate 11
Above left: Scottish Signwork
Left: NBR 4-4-0 No 256
Above: HR 4-6-0 No 103

GLASGOW

Plate 12
Above: G&SWR & SSEB
Above right: GNSR 4-4-0 No 49
Right: CR 4-2-2 No 123

33
34

35

136   The arrival of the railway on the country scene
137   required a change of attitude on certain sections of the
138   agricultural and social community; painted signs
139   which set out the new code of behaviour make
       amusing reading in these enlightened times but there
       can be no doubting the earnestness of the message.

140   The unashamed magnificence of this item of platform
       furniture, finished gilt overall, could have been inspired
       by the patron saint of all that is flamboyant in
       railway design. Saint Pancras.

141   The study of the Railway Ticket is a subject in
       itself and it is good to know that, in a museum where
       the bulk of visitors just went 'to see the engines', the
       humble Railway Ticket is not forgotten; indeed, for
       those who had time to browse, these displays opened up
       a new field of interest previously taken for granted.
       Close inspection of the exhibits would, of course, be
       essential and as one reads of journeys made long ago
       by historic Companies at unbelievable fares, a new
       insight on the railway scene is revealed. The printed
       notice which sometimes appeared on the reverse "This
       ticket is given subject to there being room on arrival

of the train, the precise hour of which will not be
positively guaranteed. No smoking allowed. No
gratuities to be given by passengers" may have some
relevance even today. Now that the familiar card
ticket 'two and a quarter inches long and one and a
quarter broad' has been ousted by automation, many
would say that the most colourful chapters in the
History of the Railway Ticket have already been
written.

142   Perhaps not the whole truth but at least something like
       the truth features on this clever GWR example.

143   Though visually very attractive, the validity of this
       LNER message could possibly be called into
       question.

144   The LMS commissioned recognised artists for the
145   Preparation of their prestige publicity material.

146   The LNER latterly concentrated on the well-earned
147   achievements of their express passenger services, a
148   policy which continued under British Railway's
149   management.

NONE BUT
COMPANY'S HORSES
ALLOWED TO DRINK
AT THIS TROUGH

MEN EMPLOYED
BY FARMERS
MUST NOT
CROSS THE MAIN LINES
TO FETCH MILK CANS

SOUTH EASTERN & CHATHAM RAILWAY.
NOTICE
TO
CABDRIVERS.

Any Cabman skylarking or
otherwise misconducting himself while on the Managing
Committee's premises or Smoking
whilst his Cab is standing
alongside the Platform will
be required to leave the
Station immediately *By Order.*

CHESHIRE LINES
NOTICE
THESE CLOSETS ARE INTENDED
FOR THE CONVENIENCE OF
PASSENGERS ONLY, WORKMEN,
CABMEN, FISHPORTERS AND
IDLERS ARE NOT PERMITTED
TO USE THEM. BY ORDER

PLACE ONE PENNY IN THE SLOT

EXHIBIT ONLY

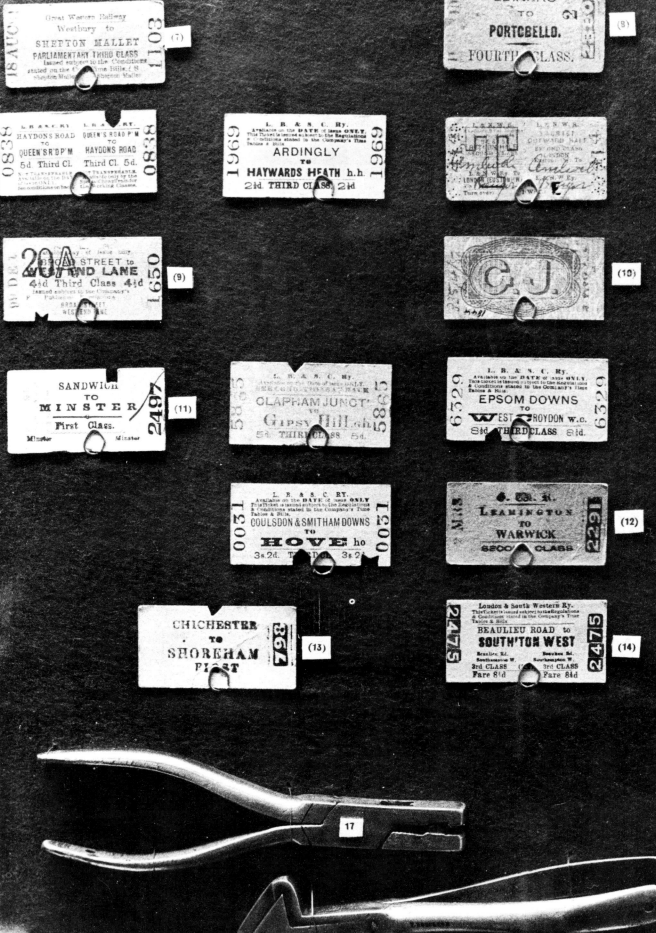

142

143

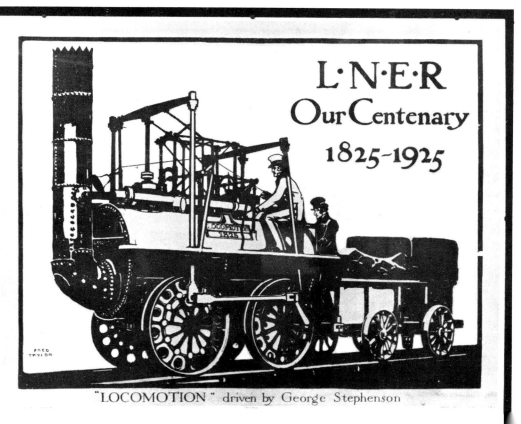

150
151
152
These excellent examples from the SR show that their posters, like their locomotives, must have raised a few eyebrows with their striking modernity.

153
154
Much of the fascination of Clapham was to be found in the writing on the walls; famous trains and famous names were brought to mind by headboards and nameplates.
'The Capitals Limited' ran between King's Cross and Edinburgh, 'The Master Cutler' between Marylebone and Sheffield and 'The Fair Maid' between London and Perth.
The nameplate Michael Faraday *is from Metropolitan Railway electric locomotive No 18,* Springbok *from LNER 4-6-0 B1 class No 1000, and* Lord Nelson *and* Sir Francis Drake *from SR 4-6-0 Lord Nelson class Nos 850 and 851.*

155
The 'Golden Arrow' service from London Victoria to Paris was one of the all-time great trains, while many ex-RAF servicemen may well remember the first time they arrived by train at Cardington or Henlow Camp.

156
A special Winston Churchill *display included the nameplate, numberplate and coat-of-arms of that famous Battle of Britain class locomotive and photographs depicted the Bulleid Pacific in Southern and British Railways liveries.*

157
J. G. Churchward *GWR 4-6-0 Castle class No 7017.*

158
Watcombe Hall *GWR 4-6-0 Hall class No 4977.*

159
Beenham Grange *GWR 4-6-0 Grange class No 6808.*

160
Earl Of Mount Edgcumbe *GWR 4-6-0 Castle class No 5043. This last nameplate was first fitted to GWR 4-4-0 Dukedog class No 3200 when built in 1936, and was later transferred to No 5043.*

161
Bachelors Button *BR 4-6-2 A2 class No 60537.*

162
North British *BR 4-6-2 A1 class No 60161.*

163
Empire Of India *LNER A4 class No 4490 later BR No 60011.*

164
Silver Fox *LNER A4 class No 2512 later BR No 60017.*

165
Exeter *SR 4-6-2 West Country class No 21C101 later BR No 34001.*

166
Torrington *SR 4-6-2 West Country class No 21C131 later BR No 34031.*

167
Spitfire *SR 4-6-2 Battle of Britain class No 21C166 later BR No 34066.*
Hurricane *SR 4-6-2 Battle of Britain class No 21C165 later BR No 34065.*

168
Sir Trafford Leigh Mallory *BR 4-6-2 Battle of Britain class No 34109.*

169
Queen Mary *LMS 4-6-2 Coronation class No 6222 later BR No 46222.*

170
The Royal Air Force *LMS 4-6-0 Royal Scot class No 6159 later BR No 46159.*

171
Duchess Of Buccleuch *LMS 4-6-2 Duchess class No 6230 later BR No 46230.*

172
Princess Helena Victoria *LMS 4-6-2 Princess class No 6208 later BR No 46208.*

Electric Locomotives
& Diesel Electric Locomotives
capable of carrying heavy goods
and passenger express trains

Progress on the
SOUTHERN RAILWAY

SOUTHERN RAILWAY

The DEVON BELLE

Fridays, Saturdays, Sundays and Mondays in each direction

dep 12.0 noon	Waterloo	arr 5.20 pm
arr 3.16 pm	Sidmouth Jct.	dep 2.3 pm
arr 3.36 pm	Exeter Ctl.	dep 1.40 pm
arr 5.32 pm	Ilfracombe	dep 12.0 noon
arr 5.36 pm	Plymouth Friary	dep 11.30 am

NEW!

ALL-PULLMAN TRAIN TO THE WEST OF ENGLAND
with Observation Car
SOUTHERN RAILWAY & PULLMAN CAR COMPANY

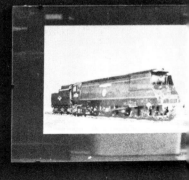

61

62

63

169 QUEEN·MARY

170 ·THE·ROYAL·AIR·FORCE·

171 DUCHESS OF BUCCLEUCH

172 ·PRINCESS· HELEN·A · VICTORIA

173 William Shakespeare BR *4-6-2 Britannia class No 70004.*

174 Oliver Cromwell BR *4-6-2 Britannia class No 70013.*

175 Clive Of India BR *4-6-2 Britannia class No 70040.*

176 Boadicea BR *4-6-2 Britannia class No 70036.*

177 Glow Worm LNWR *2-4-0 Whitworth class No 752.*
Iron Duke GWR *4-2-2 Iron Duke class never numbered.*

178 Ventnor *and* Merstone SR *0-4-4T 02 class Nos W16 and W27.*

179 Trevose Head LBSCR *4-4-2 H-2 class No 425.*
Tenterden K&ESR *2-4-0T No 1.*

180   *The age of the titled train is now, regrettably, past;*
181   *former glories are, however, recalled by this selection of locomotive headboards which bring to mind that ace of the railway pack, the 'crack express'. To identify but a few, 'The Manxman', 'The Shamrock', 'The Red Rose', 'Empress Voyager' and 'The Merseyside Express' all ran between Euston and Liverpool; 'The Irish Mail' between Euston and Holyhead; 'The Comet' and 'The Lancastrian' between Euston and Manchester; 'The Midlander' between Euston and Birmingham; 'The Royal Scot' between Euston and Glasgow/Edinburgh; 'The Lakes Express' between Euston and Keswick; 'The Northern Irishman' between St Pancras and Stranraer; 'The Mid-day Scot' between Euston and Glasgow/Edinburgh; 'The Royal Highlander' between Euston and Inverness; 'The Devonian' between Bradford and Torquay; and 'The Welshman' between Euston and Portmadoc.*

182   *The purpose of a Dynamometer Car is to assess the performance of a locomotive by measuring the drawbar pull and recording speeds, distances and fuel consumption; from this information it is possible to determine the amount of work being done by the locomotive at any given time and by relating this to the regulator and cut-off settings a measure of the mechanical efficiency is obtained. The car displayed here was built for the North Eastern Railway Company and now appears in the varnished teak of the LNER to whom ownership passed at the Grouping. In the museum it was coupled directly behind the A4 locomotive Mallard, a position it occupied on that memorable day in July 1938 when the world record for steam traction was established— a record likely to remain unbroken for all time.*

183   *The apparatus within, in gleaming brass and polished mahogany with weight and spring, disc and drum, is a symphony of complication. The electronic wizardry of the seventies could probably accomplish the same task with a transistorised device the size of a small suitcase, but we would not be impressed.*

184   *This Station Omnibus from the Garden of England entered service about the beginning of the century; it is in green and yellow livery.*

Plate 13
Above left: Dynamometer Car
Left: GER 0-6-0T No 87
Above: Hand Trolley etc

CLAPHAM

Plate 14
Above: MR *4-4-0 No 1000*
Above right: LBSCR *0-6-0T No 82*
Right: Queen Adelaide

173

174

175

76

115

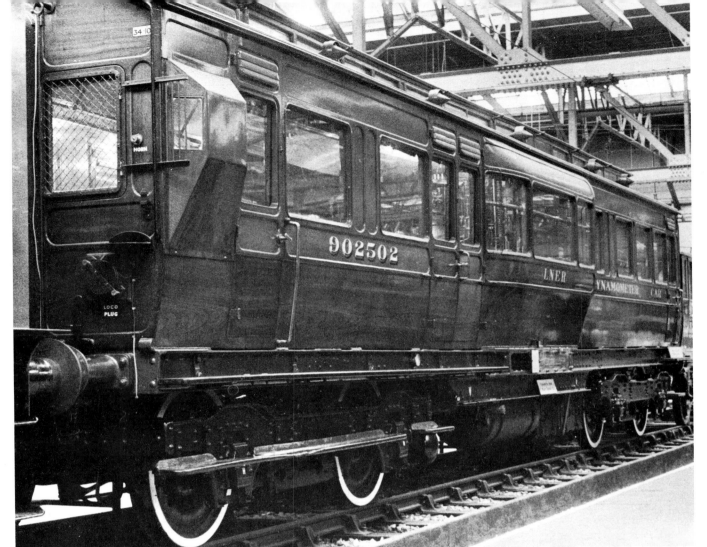

184

117

185   The Chaldron Wagon derived from the earliest
       mineral carrying vehicle in use at pit and quarry and
       continued unchanged in basic form over many years; it
       was a train of these wagons that Richard Trevithick's
       1804 locomotive hauled—though with plain wheels,
       not flanged—along the plateway on that first historic
       steam journey, and it was for the movement of wagons
       like this that the railways were first instituted. When,
       later, someone conceived the idea of carrying people by
       rail, it was in the Chaldron wagon that the first
       passengers rode—the excitement of the occasion no
       doubt compensated for the unseemly accommodation.

186   This replica of a Second Class Coach of the Liverpool
       and Manchester Railway of about 1834 shows how
       that Company provided a trim coachbuilt vehicle for
       specialist passenger services; admittedly it was without
       seats and did not have a roof but it did boast the
       thoughtful provision of drain holes in the floor to
       ensure that, in wet weather, the unfortunate passenger
       may well get soaked to the skin but would at least be
       spared the added discomfort of standing ankle deep in
       rain water.

187   The practice of naming stage coaches was carried on
188   with the railway equivalents and the railway coach
       'Traveller' is a replica of a Liverpool and
       Manchester First Class vehicle of 1834; other
       traditions of the road coach were also perpetuated,
       notably the construction and styling and the outside
       accommodation for luggage and guard (though not
       passengers) and it was to be some years before a
       distinct and separate railway coach design was to
       emerge. The interior of this replica is furnished in the
       early Victorian style and, while it would have been
       comfortable enough when stationary, it is recorded that
       it gave a hard ride and jolted passengers when
       starting.

189   The stage-coach styling is for decoration only on this
       1838 Travelling Post Office Van of the Grand
       Junction Railway, although the vehicle here is a replica
       built on a more recent chassis; in its plum and black
       livery the van incorporates the net attachment for
       collecting mail bags while at speed. Bags to be set down
       are attached to a retractable arm, barely visible
       behind the handrailing to the right of the door, which
       is then lowered at the appropriate time to engage with
       the lineside apparatus.

190   A more up-to-date variation on the TPO theme can
       be seen in the West Coast Joint Stock version in plum
       and cream livery; this vehicle is 42ft in length with
       wooden-centred wheels carried on the intriguing Webb
       radial axles. Used on England/Scotland trains, it
       was built for the London and North Western
       Railway in 1885—hence Mr Webb's influence. As the
       lineside apparatus is always positioned on the near
       side, the TPO vans require to be turned at the end of
       each run in order to conform.

191   The Midland Railway Company caused a furore in
192   the railway world in 1875 when it announced that it
193   was abolishing the Second Class; as from 1st January
       Third Class coaches were withdrawn and what had
       been Second Class stock was re-labelled Third. The
       most significant result of this was to bestow upon the
       Third Class passenger the unknown luxury of a
       padded seat, a prospect viewed with alarm by other
       railway companies all of whom agreed that Third
       class meant bare boards. Public reaction to the
       Midland decision was, of course, very favourable and
       it was inevitable that the demand for more Third
       Class accommodation should grow; one of the new
       Thirds is shown here in section and it stands as a
       memorial to a bold decision by a forward-looking
       Railway Company on a principle which was
       subsequently adopted by every other railway in the land.

189

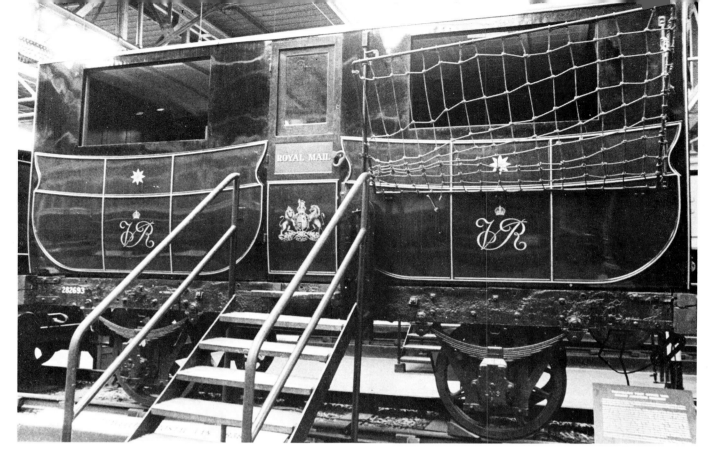

190

192

193

194
195
This is a section from an articulated pair of LNER Sleeping Cars built in 1931 which were so designed that two cars ran on three bogies, the middle bogie being placed centrally beneath the corridor connection; this arrangement had the advantage of reducing unsprung weight and facilitating maintenance. The varnished teak of this exhibit is resplendent in the exact appearance of the original and one can imagine the visual impact of a whole train of the complete coaches; it almost seems a shame that such a treat was rarely available during daylight hours. The letters and numbers, in their gold leaf with rich shadings of scarlet to pink and sober brown, exemplify the highest standards of the signwriter's art.

The nameplate Edward Thompson is from LNER A2 class Pacific No 500, later BR No 60500.

196
The Director's Saloon was an important item of rolling stock—the Admiral's Barge of the railway world—and it naturally incorporated the latest ideas in furniture and fittings. This example, from the North London Railway, was built in 1872 and boasts a varnished teak panelled exterior with decorative frosted glass borders to the windows. The vehicle is a four-wheeler carried on a timber underframe and features coal gas lighting; the North London was the first company to introduce gas lighting in its passenger coaches and was the last to convert to electricity.

197
This section is from a power car of the electric Great Northern, Piccadilly and Brompton Railway which was built in 1906 in Hungary; the vehicle later saw service on the Charing Cross, Euston and Hampstead Railway and was withdrawn from service in 1929. The section includes the original end platform ironwork and gate and featured the original non-flammable mahogany panelling on asbestos millboard specified by the fire-conscious authorities. The exterior is finished in Derby red.

198
199
The changing fortunes of fate often dictate that a vehicle is put to a use which was never envisaged by its designer, and if such an application has the effect of extending the working life of the vehicle then the result can be a happy discovery for the preservationist. This milk van, for instance, was built for the Metropolitan Railway in 1896 by the Birmingham Carriage and Wagon Company and remained in service until 1936; one can imagine that it led a hard life, and others of the batch may well have had to be withdrawn by the time this one was retired. Pure chance then brought the vehicle to the notice of the foreman of the local breakdown gang who happened to be looking for a tool van at the time, and so a tool van it became—probably with something of a farmyard flavour about it. When, years later, vehicles of outstanding historical interest were being sought for preservation the survival of this particular specimen must have been regarded as a very happy accident indeed.

194

195

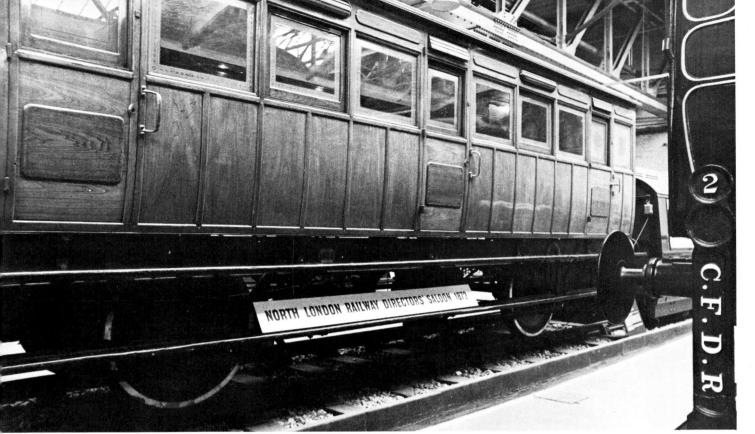

98

METROPOLITAN RAILWAY MILK VAN. 1896.

99

200 The sectioned compartment here is from the Third Corridor Standard scarlet and cream stock, designed for BR and built in the early fifties; visible in this section is the continuous curve of the bowed side from floor to guttering, with appropriate flats formed at the window apertures.

Behind can be seen the red, cream and blue liveried composite coach from the Bodmin and Wadebridge Railway; the exact date of construction is not certain but estimates put the underframe at about 1840 and the body twenty years later. The centre compartment is the First Class and the end ones, Second; it is interesting to compare the 4ft 6in width of this coach with the BR section which is around double that. The coach stood at Waterloo Station as an exhibit on one of the platforms for many years and was restored to its present condition at the Eastleigh Carriage and Wagon Works.

201 The Carriage and Wagon Works at Derby, on the other hand, were responsible for the obvious pristine condition of this Dining Carriage, No 3463 of the Midland and Glasgow and South Western Joint stock. Now resplendent in original Midland red with those lined panels that have been the despair of so many modellers, the vehicle was built at Derby in 1914 for service between London and Glasgow; it can accommodate 30 diners at one sitting of First or Third Class and the kitchen still retains its original gas ring, hot plate and cooking utensils.

202 The Pullman Car was first introduced into Britain by the Midland Railway who imported the vehicles in sections from Detroit and assembled them at the Derby Carriage and Wagon Works, the first entering service as sleepers in 1874. Later versions appeared featuring a drawing-room layout, decorated and furnished in the most expensive style of the period, and the sumptuous impression of these is well conveyed in this mock-up. Built by the Metropolitan-Cammell Carriage and Wagon Company, this exhibit illustrates the robust construction of these vehicles; the extra weight meant, of course, a heavier underframe and the resultant size of the Pullmans caused the Midland to incur the disapproval of other railway companies who feared for the safety of a train which included one of these juggernauts should there be an accident. Such fears, however, proved to be groundless and the Pullman Coach was later to be adopted throughout the land with such success that the word itself became synonymous with the highest standards of rail comfort and cuisine.

203 The Pullman Car Topaz shows the later development of this type of vehicle in the familiar brown and cream livery. Built at the Smethwick works of the Birmingham Carriage and Wagon Company in 1914, this car entered service on the South Eastern and Chatham Railway wearing crimson lake livery lined out and lettered in gold but this was changed in 1929 to the present scheme; the vehicle was withdrawn from service in 1960. Her name Topaz is no less exotic than the timbers used in her construction which include mahogany, ash, pitch pine, teak, red deal, rock elm, satin wood, tulip wood and purple wood—a rich variety indeed.

204 Visible in this panorama from left to right are the green and yellow station clock and seat, a section of a 1951 British Railways First Class compartment, the Metropolitan Railway Milk Van, the North London Railway Director's Saloon, the tender buffers of the Great Central Railway 4-4-0 and a platform ticket machine from the LNWR.

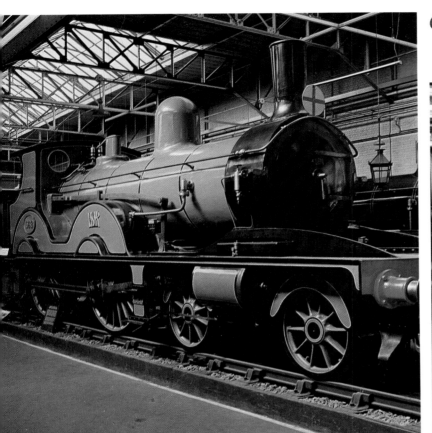

CLAPHAM

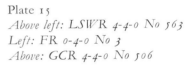

Plate 15
Above left: LSWR 4-4-0 No 563
Left: FR 0-4-0 No 3
Above: GCR 4-4-0 No 506

CLAPHAM

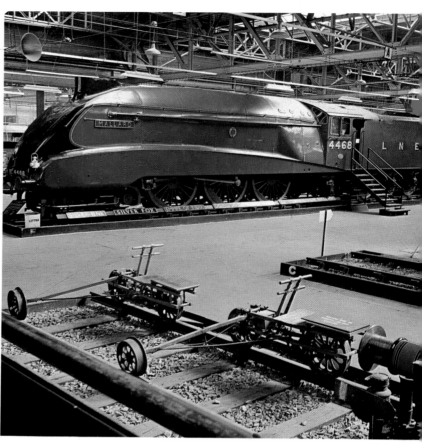

Plate 16
Above: GER 2-4-0 No 490
Above right: LNER Mallard
Right: SECR 4-4-0 No 737

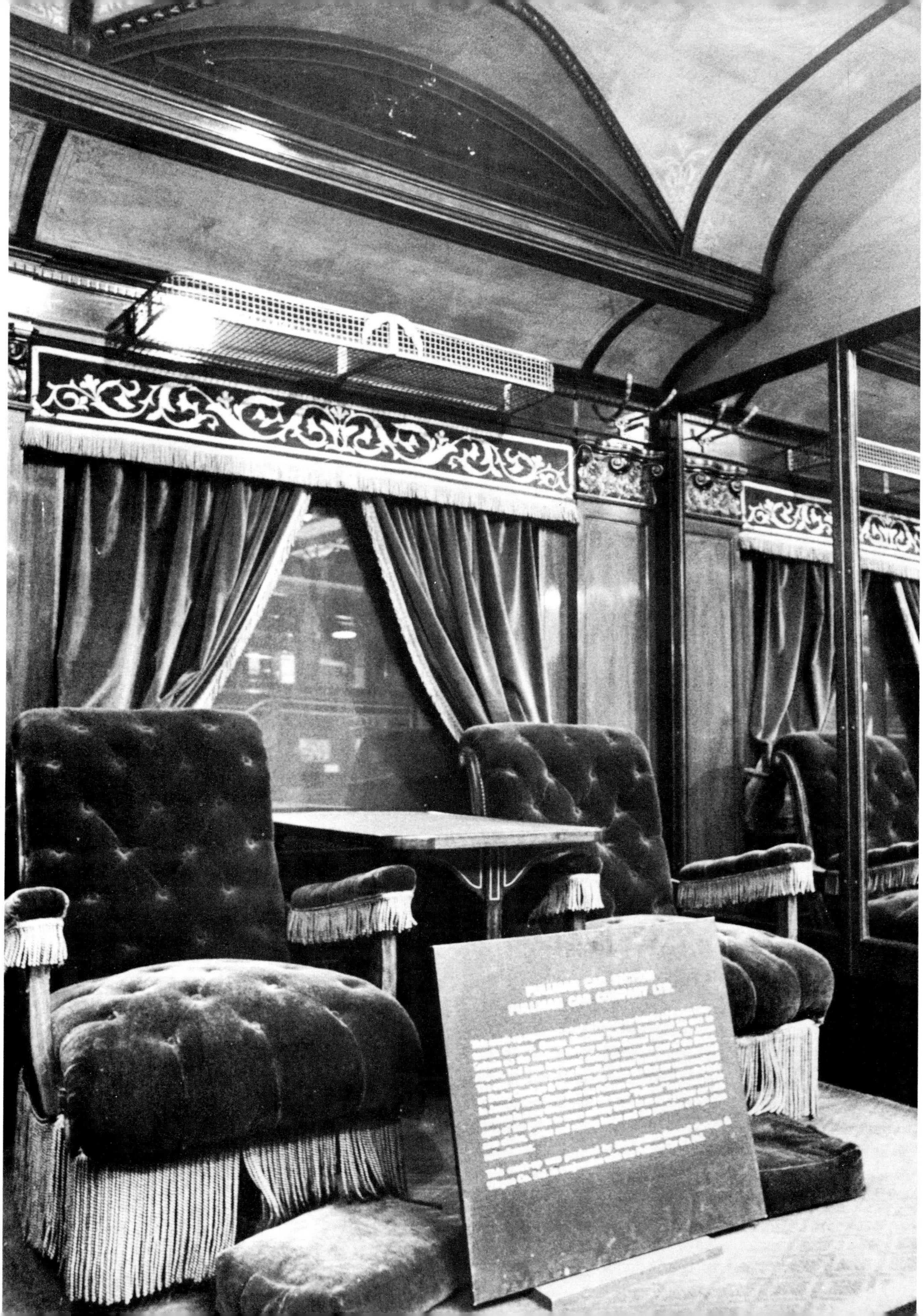

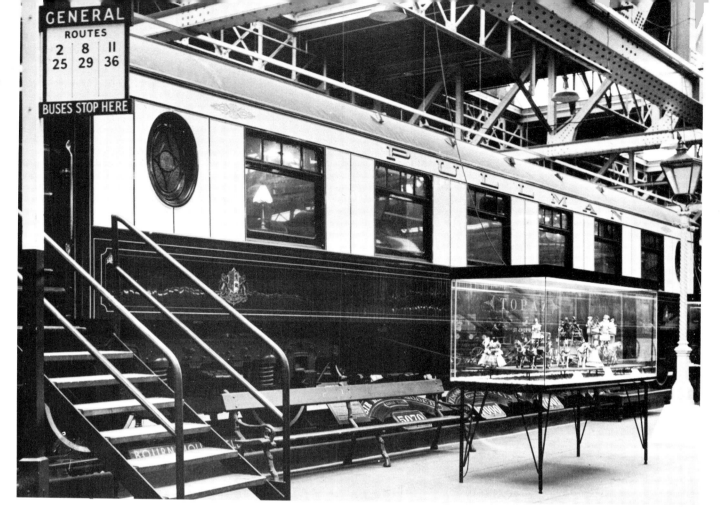

205   *The advent of the railway was the blossoming of the*
206   *communication age and all sections of the community*
207   *were to benefit from this new mobility; the industrial,*
208   *the commercial, the domestic—and the Royal. As the*
209   *sinews of iron spread throughout the land, the*
patronage of Royalty was inevitable; important
regional centres were brought to within daily travelling
distance of London and Royal attendance at provincial
functions became a practicality. The Royal estates in
the country were suddenly more accessible and the
frequent appearance of Royal Trains doubtless did
much to bolster public confidence in rail travel. The
engines of such trains were the focus of special
attention and embellishment, and this fact probably
accounts for the old Royal Train headcode where
every lamp bracket carried a lamp; the lamps
themselves received very grand styling and their shape
made them particularly suitable to carry the symbol
of Royalty. Sometimes a special headboard was
displayed, like the Great Northern example, and on
other occasions the device of the Royal personage, such
as the Prince of Wales' feathers, on the smokebox
door; large coats-of-arms were mounted on the running
plate abeam the smokebox.

210   *Queen Victoria was without doubt the gracious*
211   *monarch of the Railway Age, for it was during her*
212   *long reign that the most significant advances and*
213   *expansions in the railway system were made; within*
this period of vigorous growth, Her Majesty became a
part of an epoch of railway history that was quite
unique. Her passing was observed by railways
throughout the land and some suspended services on the
day of her funeral; the honour of carrying the late
Queen on her final journey from Paddington to
Windsor fell naturally to the Great Western Railway.
An eight coach train was marshalled and an
illuminated document lists the personages carried
therein; the engine appears to be of the Atbara class—
it carries the nameplate Royal Sovereign *and is*
numbered 3373. The wreath carried by the locomotive
is still preserved under glass and the draped coat-of-
arms illustrates the mounting of this type of device on
the running plate abeam the smokebox.

214   *This is a section of a Royal Saloon built for Queen*

Victoria at the Swindon Carriage Works of the
Great Western Railway; construction commenced in
1872 and the saloon took two years to build. Where
the interior was not padded with buttonned
upholstery it was panelled in sycamore and all furniture
was of tulip wood; the side framing was of mahogany
and the underbody oak. Sound insulation on the floor
was provided by pile carpets laid on felt beneath
which three hundred pieces of cork were laid on the
double diagonal floorboards. The connecting doors
carried bevelled mirrors to increase the apparent
interior length.

215   *The London and North Western Railways Wolverton*
Carriage Works produced a Royal Coach for King
Edward and later an externally similar vehicle for
Queen Alexandra; the coaches differed in interior
layout but they were designed to be run as a pair and
form the nucleus of a Royal Train. The splendid
vestibule double doors are of baronial proportions;
below them can be seen the folding platform steps.
The crown visible in the centre is an item of railway
regalia and has no connection with the adjacent
nameplate Sir William A. Stanier F.R.S. *which is*
from the LMS Duchess class Pacific No 6256,
later BR No 46256.

216   *Also hailing from Wolverton Works is Queen*
217   *Victoria's London and North Western Railway*
Saloon built in 1895. Originally constructed in 1869
as a pair of carriages connected by an enclosed
flexible gangway, an innovation on the railway scene
and a LNWR 'first', the two were due to be
replaced by a completely new vehicle. However, Her
Majesty had formed quite a liking for the old saloons
and so they were retained but mounted together on a
single underframe and placed on two six-wheeled
bogies; in this form the vehicle ran until the great
Queen died since when it has been preserved in the
condition in which she last used it. The livery, contrary
to normal LNWR practice, is plum and white with
gold lining and, in addition to the Royal Arms,
features the badges of the Orders of the Bath, the
Thistle, the Garter and St Patrick; the spring leaves
are picked out in alternate colours and the gilded lion
heads add the final touch of pageantry.

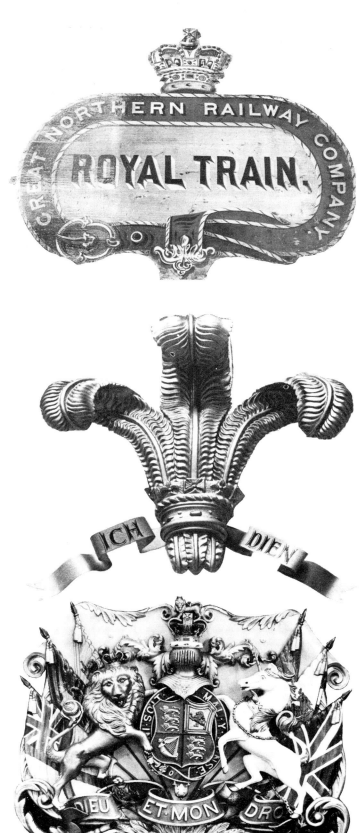

North Eastern Railway.

DISCONTINUANCE OF TRAINS.

FUNERAL OF HER LATE MAJESTY

QUEEN VICTORIA,

On SATURDAY, 2nd February, 1901.

THE Ordinary train service will be suspended, and the Sunday service will be substituted, except on certain portions of the line, for particulars of which see bills exhibited at the Stations.

YORK. January, 1901.   GEORGE S. GIBB, General Manager.

BEN JOHNSON & CO., PRINTERS, YORK.

WREATH CARRIED ON FRONT OF ENGINE "ROYAL SOVEREIGN" WHICH DREW THE TRAIN THAT CONVEYED THE BODY OF THE LATE QUEEN VICTORIA FROM PADDINGTON TO WINDSOR ON FEBRUARY 2ND 1901.

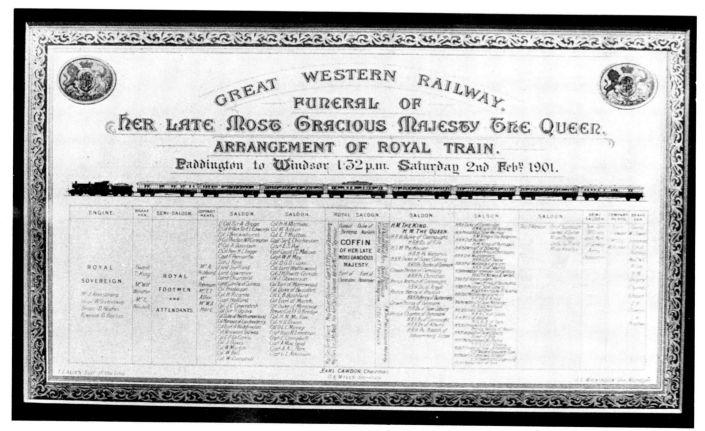

SECTION OF ROYAL SALOON
GREAT WESTERN RAILWAY

SIR WILLIAM A. STANIER, F.R.

218 The Duke of Sutherland's Private Saloon was also built at Wolverton by the London and North Western Railway and was, in fact, used as a prototype for later Royal Saloons. Accommodation comprises a large saloon, with figured lincrusta roof in white and gold, a small compartment, two sleeping berths and associated toilet facilities and a pantry with cooking stove; the exterior is finished in dark green with cream upper panels lined in gold and all doors are varnished. Throughout the LNWR and LMS days the coach was used privately by the owner and was the last one to be run—after Nationalisation such privileges were withdrawn.

219 Royal Coach interiors glimpsed from the adjacent
220 elevated staging show the writing desk of Queen Alexandra's Saloon and a floral arrangement in Queen Victoria's Saloon.

221 More interior views of Royal Coaches show, top, the
222 day room of Queen Victoria's Saloon where the sumptuous upholstery and roof lining can be seen; beyond is the tender of the SECR 4-4-0 locomotive. The lower photograph shows the sleeping compartment of Queen Alexandra's Saloon; side windows carry a decorative frosted design incorporating the badges of the Orders of St Patrick, left, and the Thistle, right. Through the clear centre window can be seen the

nameplate from LMS 4-6-0 locomotive No 5737 Atlas, one end of Queen Victoria's Saloon and, in the distance, the front end of Mallard; reflected in the dressing table mirror is none other than King Henry VIII who appears on a poster on the wall behind.

223 In 1842 the London and Birmingham Railway built this Royal Coach for Queen Adelaide Amelia Louisa Caroline who married King William IV in 1818. The coach was an elaboration of the standard First Class coach and was constructed at the Euston Works using a coach-built body. The compartment at the near end has folding seats converting to a bed which would have been rather cramped were it not for the box-like extension at the end, placed thus to accommodate the Royal feet; at the far end is a half compartment in which attendants would ride. The immaculate livery is of deep claret and black with gold trim and gold plated door handles.

224 In this photograph can be seen the two and a half compartment layout of the coach and the elevated walkway which also serves to display prints and a carriage carpet from the Metropolitan Railway. The nameplates Cochrane and Hogue are from LMS 4-6-0 Jubilee class locomotives Nos 5656 and 5683 respectively.

225 *Looking as if it really is thundering down the line is this model of a very famous locomotive. The copper capped chimney gives a clue to the Great Western origins of the engine but it is the bell on the buffer beam that really identifies it; there is no need to put the number 6000 on the front —*Kinge George V *is too well known to need that. The bell commemmorates the 1927 visit to the USA by* King George V *and the* North Star *replica to attend the Baltimore and Ohio Railway Centenary; the actual locomotive, the first of its class, is preserved in running order to this day.*

226 *Reflections in the glass, and objects beyond, give a surrealistic appearance to this picture of the Great Eastern Railway 4-4-0 locomotive No 1900* Claud Hamilton; *the model perpetuates the memory of one of the most successful class of 4-4-0 express passenger locomotives ever built. Named after the Chairman of the GER, No 1900 was the only one to carry a name but others of the class, some of which remained in service for 50 years, were always referred to as 'Claud Hamiltons'.*

227 *When original locomotives have long since disappeared or where the space to store them is simply not available, re-creation in miniature is made possible by the skill and patience of the model builder. In this example the only feature that distinguishes the model from the real thing is the size of the bolt heads—that apart, the actual 4-6-0 LMS locomotive could be standing before you.*

228 *A certain similarity between the object of the lower*

photograph and Columbine *at the York Museum may be detected. Both are Allan designs for the Grand Junction Railway and built at Crewe around 1845;* Columbine *was the 2-2-2 passenger locomotive while the 2-4-0 design modelled here was the goods engine.*

229 *The picture shows a model of the London and South Western Railway locomotive No 580 of Adams's 4-4-0 X2 class; the original had 7ft 1in diameter driving wheels and from it derived the T3 class with 6ft 7in diameter driving wheels.*

230 *The legendary Richard Trevithick, that quiet Cornishman who was intrigued by steam engines, who invented the steam locomotive and who left the country to seek his fortune abroad, is commemmorated here by a model of his most famous creation, the Pen-y-Daren locomotive of 1804. Having built a high-pressure steam engine, a road locomotive and a steam passenger coach, Trevithick accepted a commission from an individual who had made a bet with a friend that a steam locomotive could be made to haul a load. At the Pen-y-Daren Colliery in South Wales Trevithick built his machine and put it to the test—the outcome was successful and the bet was won. Stimulated, Trevithick went on to build several more locomotive types—one,* Black Billy *went to Tyneside while another* Catch-me-who-can *was demonstrated in London in 1808—but he received neither support nor encouragement and therefore turned his attention elsewhere. It was to be one of the Tynesiders who saw* Black Billy *at work who was to further Trevithick's ideals to fruition—his name was Robert Stephenson.*

30

231 To list and describe the large number of O-gauge
232 models on display is not practicable but examples are
233 shown here of locomotives, passenger coaches and goods
stock of all periods and regions. The method of
display, against background enlargements of
contemporary prints, was worthy of mention and
suitably recalls the railway scene of long ago.

234 In the early days before railway companies were
235 sufficiently large (or secure) to support their own
236 works, there were several manufacturer's of locomotives
who produced motive power 'off the peg'. One of these
was the Liverpool firm of Bury Curtiss and Kennedy
(later to become W. Fairburn) who built, for the
most part, small locomotives of the 0-4-0 or 2-2-0
types weighing under 20 tons. Around 1845 the
Furness Railway purchased four of the 0-4-0 engines
and No 3 of this batch served for 54 years in that
most attractive north-west corner of England before
being retired and placed on permanent display inside a
large glass case on Barrow Station. World War II
brought heavy air attacks on the shipbuilding
installations of Barrow and during one of these the
station was hit and Old Coppernob, as No 3 had
become known, was damaged and made homeless.
Fortunately, swift removal to Horwich works
prevented further deterioration and later restoration
to her former glory of iron-ore red preceeded her
installation at Clapham; there, still bearing the
evidence of her war-wounds, her domed copper boiler
perpetuates the memory of a famous locomotive
builder and a famous railway.

237 This is another instance where a locomotive has
238 survived in a form vastly different from that in which
239 it originally appeared. While there is some doubt as to
240 the wheel arrangement, 2-2-2 or 4-2-2, Francis
Trevithick turned out the original No 173 Cornwall
for the London and North Western Railway at
Crewe in 1847 with the 8ft 6in diameter driving
wheels it still retains, but with the unusual feature of
having the boiler carried below the driving axle, down
between the frames. The physical restrictions on
boiler size imposed by other running gear severely
limited its steaming capacity—though one point in
favour of such an arrangement would have been the
unrivalled visibility from the footplate—and so the
locomotive was rebuilt by Ramsbottom in 1858 with
a more conventional layout and later renumbered 3020.
Webb added further refinements in 1871, including a
standard chimney, closed in safety valves and a cab,
and the locomotive acquired its present form in 1887
with the fitting of a new boiler and a circular
smokebox door. No 3020 ran in ordinary service until
1902 but it was later returned to work to haul the
Chief Mechanical Engineers' Saloon on official
LNWR business; final retirement came in 1922.

241 Nowadays it is not easy to imagine a steam-worked
242 underground railway but, of course, such a system did
243 exist in London for many years and laid the
foundation for the fast, clean, frequent electric
operation we know today. One of the best known of
underground locomotives first appeared in 1864 from
the works of Beyer-Peacock and, from a total batch
of 66 built for the Metropolitan Railway, No 23 is
the last survivor; the locomotive is fitted with simple
condensing apparatus and the junction above the
cylinders incorporates a valve to direct the exhaust
steam either into the smokebox or along the large
pipes to the tanks depending on whether running on
the surface or underground. Locomotives of this class
carried the brunt of underground traffic for 40 years
until the changeover to electricity which began in
1903; No 23 was built in 1866, rebuilt in 1889,
1903 and 1918 and spent the twilight of its career
out in the countryside on the Brill Branch in
Metro-land. It ended its days working engineers'
trains on the Metropolitan and District Lines of
London Transport and was withdrawn from service
in 1948 to be restored to its 1903 form in the wine
coloured Metropolitan livery.

31

METROPOLITAN RAILWAY LOCOMOTIVE Nº 23. 1866

244   The firm of Aveling and Porter is more usually
245   associated with the manufacture of traction engines
246   and steam rollers and so, when that company turns
247   out railway locomotives, one can expect certain visual
     similarities; looking at locomotive No 807, one is not
     disappointed. One of a pair built in 1872 for the
     Wotton Tramway in Buckinghamshire, No 807
     weighs under 10 tons and cost £400: it entered
     service on the estate line of the Duke of Buckingham
     and, probably due to some peculiarity of the chain
     drive, proved to be a better performer when running
     chimney first. When the line was extended to Brill,
     turntables were therefore provided at each end and the
     whole enterprise was taken over by the Oxford and
     Aylesbury Tramroad in 1894 (later to become the
     Brill Branch of the Metropolitan Railway in 1899),
     when No 807 was acquired by a company that
     rejoiced in the name of the Blisworth and Stowe
     Brick and Tile Company of Nether Heyford,
     Northants. When the brickworks closed in 1940 the
     locomotive lay derelict for some ten years until the
     Industrial Locomotive Society rescued it and
     presented it to the British Transport Commission;
     restoration took place at Neasden with the co-operation
     of Messrs Aveling Barford and No 807 is now the
     unique survivor of a very unusual locomotive type.

248   The 'Brighton Terriers' of William Stroudley became
249   a legend in their own lifetime, if only for the reason
250   that their lifetime was such a long one. Production
251   started at the Brighton Works of the London,
     Brighton and South Coast Railway in 1872 and
     examples were still to be found in service with
     British Railways some ninety years later. From a
     total of fifty originally built about ten have been
     preserved; No 82 Boxhill represents the class here
     beautifully restored to that most attractive golden
     ochre with which the LBSCR will always be
     associated. This particular company was most
     enthusiastic to name locomotives and hand-painted
     names, applied to tank sides or splashers, read like a

gazetteer of Sussex and the south—occasionally to the
confusion of those passengers who took them for
destination indicators. Boxhill was built in 1880 for
working the East London Railway between New
Cross and Liverpool Street and on the South London
line between Victoria and London Bridge, but went
on to spend many years as locomotive shunter at the
Brighton Works. Withdrawn from service in 1947
and fully restored at Eastleigh Works, Southampton,
it is comforting to know that such a splendid
example is available to recall what was probably the
most popular 0-6-0T locomotive ever to enter service.

252   Standing by the water column, and its associated
253   drain cover and brazier, is the locomotive Hardwicke,
254   No 790 of the London and North Western
     Railway Precedent class. This Webb 2-4-0 class,
     along with the Precursors and the Whitworths (130
     locomotives in all) were the mainstays of the LNWR
     passenger fleet for the half-century preceeding the
     Grouping, and the last one in service, No 5001
     Snowdon of the Precedent class was not in fact
     withdrawn until 1934. The rate of growth of this
     locomotive stud is said to have caused some disquiet
     among the shareholders of the LNWR and so, the
     story goes, a ruse was employed to give the impression
     that production was not running as high as it actually
     was; thus, Hardwicke which was built in 1892
     carries on its nameplate the inscription 'Crewe 1873'.
     Whether or not this subterfuge had the desired effect
     is not recorded but the Precedents went on to
     distinguish themselves with many notable performances;
     in the 1895 Race to the North No 790 itself
     hustled its train from Crewe to Carlisle at an
     average speed of 67.2mph, clocking a 74.5mph
     average on the final Penrith to Carlisle stretch. The
     locomotive became LMS No 5031 at the Grouping
     and thus continued to run until withdrawal in 1932
     when the paint shop at Crewe Works gave Hardwicke
     a temporary home for 30 years before coming to the
     museum.

44

45

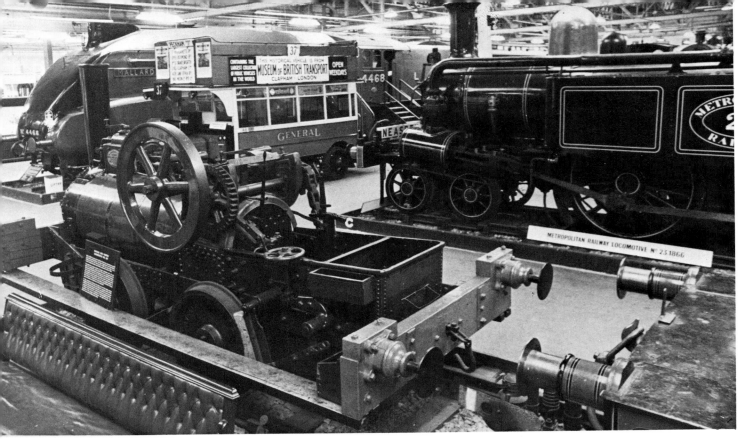

255
256
257 At a time when other locomotive designers were attempting to improve performance by the application of compounding or with the assistance of the fashionable gadgetry of the day, William Adams at the Nine Elms Works of the London and South Western Railway decided to start at square one and design a locomotive from the regulator outwards; every attention was paid to the stage by stage progress of the steam right up to the time it passed out of the chimney. Sound basic design was followed up by superb workmanship and the result was a free-steaming passenger locomotive, the most powerful in Britain at the time, which made short work of the West Country expresses it was called upon to work. Stemming from the X2 class, of which 30 were built with 7ft 1in diameter driving wheels, came the 30 examples of the T3 class with 6ft 7in diameter driving wheels; No 563 is an 1893 example of the latter and the attractive front end which was common to both classes features a stovepipe chimney and a 7ft 6in bogie wheelbase. This locomotive was withdrawn in 1939 but was 'called-up' again for the duration of the war, to be demobilised at Eastleigh and await the restoration which was to come in 1948 for exhibition at the Waterloo Centenary.

258 The model by the tender is of the LMS 2-6-0+0-6-2 Beyer Garratt No 4972, one of a class of 33 articulated locomotives built for the coal traffic between Nottingham and London; the model is the work of apprentices at Crewe.

259
260 Locomotive No 490 of the Great Eastern Railway represents James Holden's 2-4-0 T26 or Intermediate class introduced in 1891; 90 examples of the class were turned out from the Stratford Works between then and 1896. This class developed from the larger T19 class, some of which were converted for oil-burning, and the two classes between them were the backbone of the Great Eastern's mixed traffic fleet for over 50 years. No 490 was built in 1894 and ran under a variety of numbers; at the Grouping it became LNER No 7490, in 1942 it was renumbered No 7802 and again in 1946 to No 2785. British Railways issued the number 62785 at Nationalisation and this remained unchanged until the locomotive ended its days in the Cambridge area in 1959, usually working to Colchester or Mildenhall, along with two others of the class (both of which had non-original side window cabs fitted in 1936) as the last 2-4-0s in BR service. The complete and thorough restoration was carried out at Stratford Works and the open smokebox door allows study of the spark arrester grid and the long blast pipe which sports the refinement of a Macallan variable orifice.

59

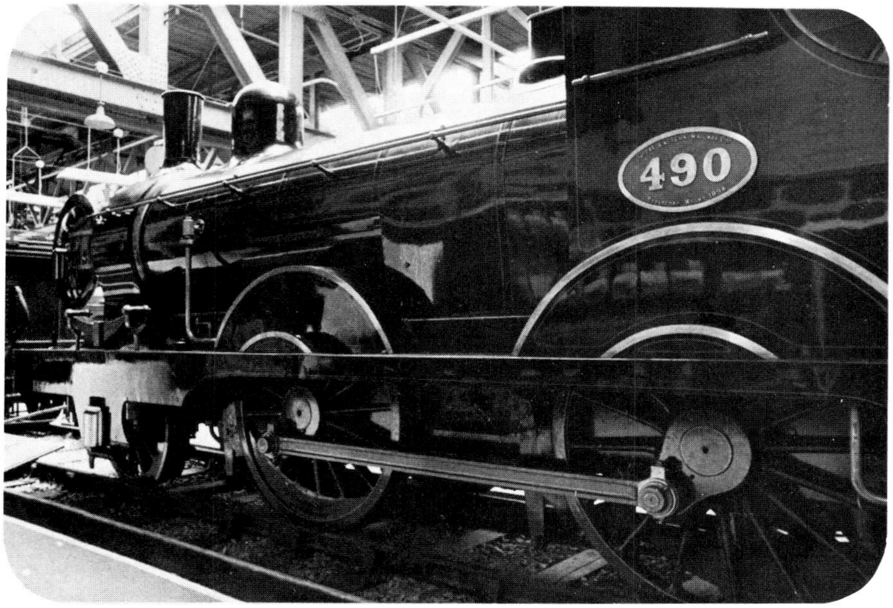

o

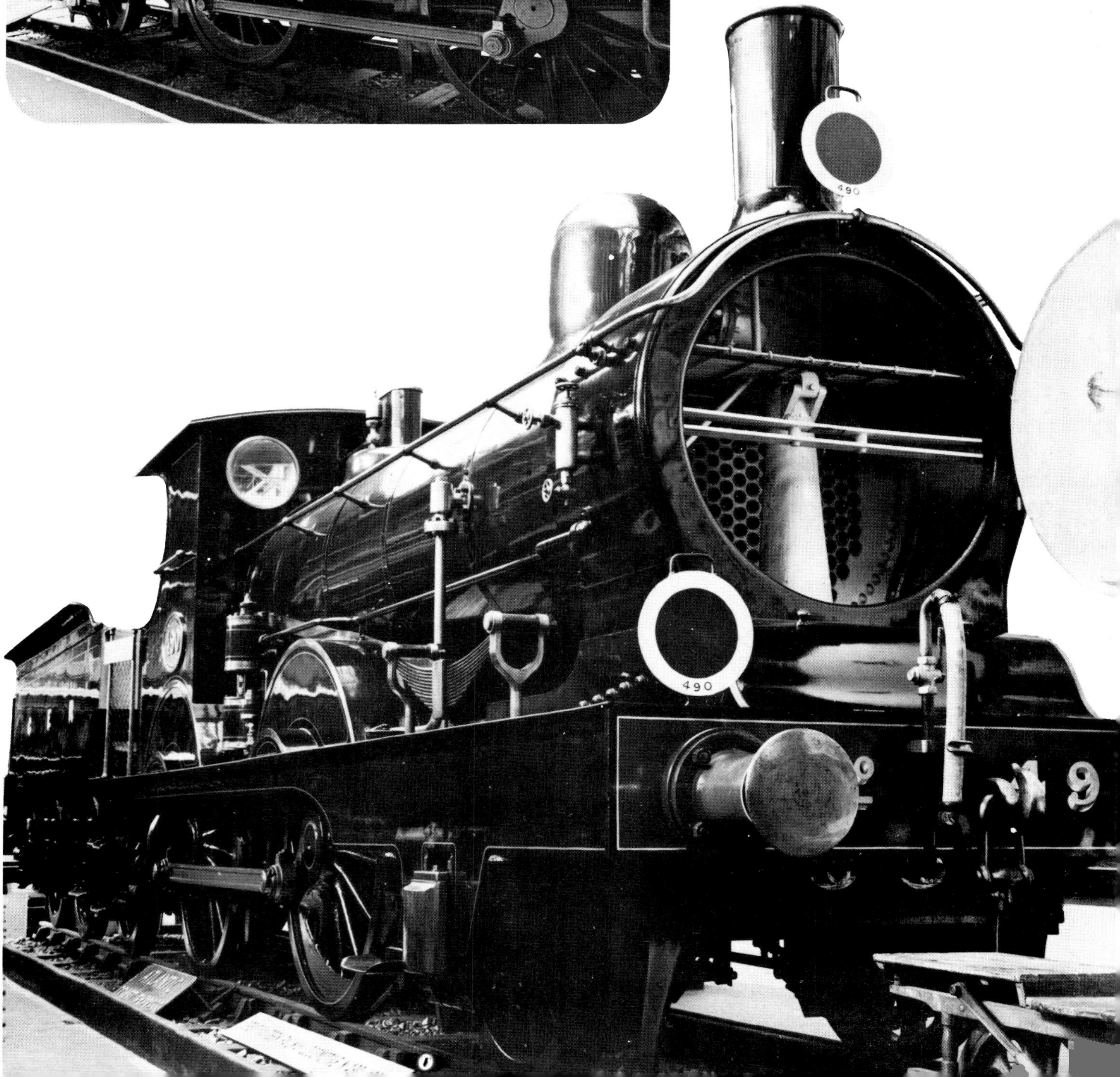

261 Yet another example of ideal proportion and perfect
262 line is Harry Wainwright's D class design for the
263 South Eastern and Chatham Railway 4-4-0
264 locomotive of 1901; 'handsome is as handsome does'
and the performance of these beauties on the heavy
boat trains in the early part of the century made them
an outstanding class. Derived from the M3 class of
the London, Chatham and Dover Railway (a company
which amalgamated with the South Eastern Railway
in 1899 to become the SECR) the D class locomotives
were built in 1901 at the Ashford (Kent) Works and
were responsible for the heavy haulage on the
company's routes until the outbreak of World War I;
many were rebuilt by Maunsell with superheaters. No
737, at the Grouping, became Southern Railway No
A737, later No 1737, and BR No 31737 at
Nationalisation, to be withdrawn in 1956 and restored
to former glory in 1960. The brass rimmed splashers
swoop and soar in curving grace and, from its brass
dome and chimney rim to its decorated tender
axleboxes, it is surely one of the most splendid
locomotives ever to ride the rails.

265 Differing somewhat from its original appearance is
266 the Midland Compound which stands as a reminder of
one of the adventure stories in the history of the
development of the locomotive. Steam exhausted from a
cylinder still retains some of its expansive properties
and it is to utilise this otherwise wasted energy that
provides the reason for compounding; in this example,

steam from the regulator first operates a smaller
high-pressure cylinder between the frames and is then
fed to the two low-pressure outside cylinders. The
system does make very efficient use of the steam,
making for economical operation, but it is at the
expense of more complicated machinery and added
maintenance; for instance, in No 1000, all three
cylinders drive the same axle and this involves three
sets of Stephenson's valve gear operated by six
eccentrics on one axle. However, the Midland Railway
decided on a compound 4-4-0 using Smith's system
and Johnson built five locomotives in 1902 at Derby
which were later to be rebuilt by Henry Fowler during
World War I; another followed in 1905, having been
modified by Deeley who had by then succeeded Johnson,
and this version was rebuilt in improved form in
1923 to be followed by 39 others. Superheating was
incorporated from 1913 onwards and after the
Grouping a further 195 examples were built and the
class went on to distinguish itself as the only really
successful British compound locomotive. The 'Crimson
Ramblers', as they became known, are represented by
the Midland splendour of No 2631 built in 1902;
renumbered MR 1000 in 1907, the locomotive
retained that number throughout its LMS career until
becoming BR No M1000 with Nationalisation. It
was again renumbered BR No 41000 in 1949,
withdrawn in 1951, restored in 1959 and used on
enthusiasts' specials before being transferred to the
museum in 1962.

MIDLAND RAILWAY LOCOMOTIVE Nº 1000. 1902

267
268
The Great Eastern Railway suburban service from Liverpool Street Station was the most intensive steam operated service in the world at the time, and the achievement of this distinction owed much to the willingness and reliability of the 230 strong P57 class of sturdy 0-6-0 tank locomotives. Holden derived the design from his R24 class of 1890 and, with a higher boiler pressure, larger water tanks, Westinghouse brakes and screw reversing gear, came up in 1902 with a maid-of-all-work equally at home on shunting duties and suburban passenger trains alike. These trains, incidentally, played a colourful part in the pageant of railway history; as the frequency of service was stepped up, improvements in passenger handling were necessitated and so; instead of having the class indicated by a figure on the carriage door, the doors themselves were painted in identifying colours overall and thus was born their nickname 'The Jazz Trains'. No 87 is a survivor from the later class and was built in 1904 at the Stratford Works of the GER; after the Grouping it was given LNER No 7087 but in 1946 became No 8633. Nationalisation brought BR No 68633 and the locomotive was withdrawn in 1959; restoration to the pristine original livery of the GER was undertaken at Stratford.

'The Cornishman' headboard recalls a titled train of the Great Western Railway instituted in the broad gauge days on the Paddington to Penzance run, though latterly the title was given to a train running from Wolverhampton to Penzance; above the name a colourful Cornish Piskey vaults over a toadstool.

269
270
271
272
J.G. Robinson of the Great Central Railway designed some fine locomotives of the 4-4-2, 4-4-0 and 4-6-0 types with massive boilers and particularly handsome lines. It was found that, with the application of superheating, a 4-4-0 could do the work of an Atlantic and the D10 class of 10 locomotives followed by the 11 D11 class were introduced on this basis; these could then work between London and Manchester direct whereas the Atlantics had to be changed en route. The first ten were named after directors of the GCR and, while this policy obtained for some of the eleven which followed, others were given names to commemmorate Royal personages and World War I battles; the Hon Eric Butler-Henderson was a director of the Company, and later of the LNER, and No 506 carries his name. This locomotive was built at the Gorton Works in 1919 and allocated to the depot at Neasden; at the Grouping it became LNER No 5506 and in 1946 No 2660, while Nationalisation brought BR No 62660. During the LNER days one small styling change was made when the smaller splashers on the running plate were removed, presumably to facilitate access to the coupling rods; happily they were replaced during restoration.

273   One of the more fascinating industrial locomotives is
274   the 0-4-0 Wren built by Beyer-Peacock for service at
      the Horwich Works of the Lancashire and
      Yorkshire Railway. Wren was one of the first three
      built in 1887 for the works tramway; eight locomotives
      were built altogether for light haulage duties moving a
      variety of items ranging from locomotive parts and
      materials to the weekly wages—and one would not be
      surprised at the tea trolley as well. The other seven
      examples were named, delightfully, Bee, Fly, Wasp,
      Midget, Mouse, Robin and Dot, all of which have
      now gone save Dot, on loan to the Narrow Gauge
      Railway Museum at Towyn. The dimensions of these
      locomotives are as intriguing as their appearance;
      gauge 1ft 6in, driving wheel diameter 1ft 4½in, weight
      3 tons, 11 cwt 2 qrs, boiler pressure 170lb/sq in and
      cylinders 5in diameter by 6in stroke. Wren worked
      until 1957 and then spent six years as a standby for
      its diesel replacement; it now appears in the original
      black livery of the Lancashire and Yorkshire Railway
      lined out in red and white, the colours of the county
      roses.
      Behind the diminutive Wren stands mighty Mallard.

275   Sir Nigel Gresley built four of the streamlined A4
276   class Pacifics to inaugurate the LNER 'Silver
277   Jubilee' service from Newcastle to London in 1935,
278   the test train making its trial run on 27th September,
279   110 years to the day after George Stephenson first
280   drove Locomotion on the Stockton and Darlington
281   Railway metals. The first four were liveried in silver
      grey, to match the special coaches which had a similar
      finish and sported stainless steel trim, and were named
      Silver Link, Silver King, Quicksilver and
      Silver Fox. At a time when 'streamlined' aircraft
      were replacing the old biplanes, the idea of a
      streamlined train really took public imagination by
      storm and within a very short time the glittering
      'Silver Jubilee' became the most famous train in the
      land; if it was sensational in appearance it was no
      less sensational in performance. Newcastle departure
      10am, Kings Cross arrival 2pm; Kings Cross
      departure 5.30pm, Newcastle arrival 9.30pm.
      Running Monday to Friday with a surcharge of 5/- for
      First Class and 3/- for Third, so great was public
      support that the cost of building the train was
      recovered completely by the surcharge alone within the
      first two years of operation.

Streamlined casing apart, the locomotives incorporated
the ultimate refinements in Doncaster Pacific design,
such as a 250lb/sq in boiler pressure, larger diameter
piston valves, and internally streamlined steam
passages (with double chimneys to come) and thirty
more examples, turned out in garter blue, were to
appear over the next three years. These were named,
for the most part, after sea birds and wild fowl; a
few names honoured Commonwealth countries and
there were several re-namings later to commemmorate
prominent personalities. If the seven-coach 'Silver
Jubilee' had astonished the experts, there was more to
come, for a new train of nine coaches 'The Coronation'
was to bring Edinburgh to within six hours of London;
this target was set with the A4s in mind and their
subsequent performance proved them to be outstanding
locomotives indeed.
One operational procedure that had been found
necessary with the new expresses was that signal
working had to be carried out two blocks ahead
instead of the usual one and, consequent upon this, it
was decided to carry out trials in 1938 to evaluate
a new quick-setting brake which could have the effect
of reducing stopping distances. These trials involved
the inclusion of a Dynamometer Car in addition to
the train of six coaches and it was in the course of one
southbound run between Grantham and Peterborough
on 3rd July 1938 that the world record speed of
126mph was recorded. At the head of the train was
locomotive No 4468, the immortal Mallard.
The news was broadcast to the world that Britain
ruled the rails and this spectacular achievement was
observed by presenting laurels to Mallard which
adorn the boiler sides to this day. Fourteen months
later the event became overshadowed by the clouds of
war; the A4s were repainted sombre black and, to
facilitate maintenance, were stripped of the curved
valance plate over the valve gear. With
Nationalisation the class appeared in BR green and
ten years later were facing extinction, displaced by the
Deltics and relegated in the early sixties to such
unglamorous duties as the Aberdeen fish trains—it
was a sad passing.
To the observer with any imagination, however, the
excitement of that proud moment in history can be
recaptured for a while as one surveys each flowing line
and every intricate detail of Mallard the magnificent.

73

74